Caugh

RIPtıae

Caught in a RIPtide
by author Judy Condie
© Judy Condie, 2024

All Illustrations by Robin Hunter
© Robin Hunter, 2024

Edited by Daniel Bingham
© Daniel Bingham, 2024

Book design by Tessie Sangha
© Tessie Sangha, 2024

A CIP catalogue record for this book is available at the British Library.

ISBN: 978-1-3999-9330-2

Caught in a
RIPtide

Dedications

To my dearest Richard,
without whom I wouldn't be mother to Catherine,
Michael and Nicholas, my saviours.

Remembering my lovely smiling Mum, you and Dad
were my bedrock. Thank you.

Missing my beautiful Jet and his loyal company.

A partner, a parent or a pet. Their love is at the very
heart of our lives. Treasure them.

Foreword

Caught in a RIPtide

Progression: 'the process of developing or moving gradually towards a more advanced state'.

*The word progression has **two** meanings in cancer.*

The good stuff being research, trials, constant testing, new data, fund raising, endless marketing and advertising, with regular updates and encouraging results and the word cancer becoming acceptable in everyday speak. This all means less heartache, less pain, and more hope for all those involved with the treatments.

The bad stuff is when you have cancer, it is not a word you want to hear. It means tumours have either grown or stopped reacting to treatment, reducing the chances of further action. Another drug may be offered with different risks and side effects to manage and new terminology that keeps you constantly on a knife edge.

At the beginning of the journey, you know absolutely nothing about any of this, without previous experience it is a minefield in a frightening, exclusive world of unbridled emotion, wakeful nights, nervous chats, dark humour and the searching of unfamiliar words online every time a report comes through the post, desperate for an answer and a miracle cure.

I do not even have cancer, but my husband did.

Without the first description of the word progression, the second one would, most certainly, be far more common and destructive which is why I am personally so grateful for all the work, time and commitment displayed by cancer research teams, particularly in our case, the Royal Marsden Hospital.

Without them we would not be several years on from that first unforgettable day, so thank you.

This is my story, as a helpless onlooker, of my own emotional, physical and geographical journey.

May you all be able to progress with the good stuff in order to reduce the bad stuff.

Chapter 1

The Take Off

The view from the aeroplane window, slightly misaligned with my seat, was spoiled by scratches on the inner, plastic pane. I often bumped my head against it while trying to get a closer look at the vast world far below, rendered miniature. I wondered how the scratches came to be – had previous passengers clawed their fears into the perspex?

Regardless, this thwarted my attempt to capture a clear photograph of my favourite view: the cotton wool horizon stretching endlessly, crowned by a perfect, blue sky and perpetual sunshine, with sporadic patches of land and sea. I felt honoured to see parts of the earth from such heights, coastlines and rivers unseen from the ground, all resembling a meticulously crafted model village. The clouds appeared solid, like snow-covered mountains within reach, though I knew they would simply dissolve like mist in my hands upon touch.

Sitting inside the airport lounge with only my breakfast for company, I felt caught between worlds. Outside, the runway buzzed with activity, each departure and arrival sending my heart into my mouth when I dared to look. Airports are strange places, full of people with planned destinations and reasons significant enough to warrant flying. Some visit family, others start new jobs, chase sunshine, or simply crave a break from the routine of everyday life. The rush through security checkpoints, the unaccustomed sight of high street shops, or the temptation of a ridiculously early drink at the bar are all part of the experience.

The long walk to the gates, the relief when a screaming toddler peels off to a different one, and the anticipation of meeting fellow passengers are all familiar rituals. As I join the boarding queue, I can't help but wonder who my immediate neighbour will be for the next 17 hours. Will we exchange pleasantries, or avoid eye contact? The thought of bumping elbows and exchanging awkward requests to squeeze by for the toilet have me praying for an empty seat or, at least, an agreeable fellow traveller. They may be someone whose incessant, loud snoring will keep me awake, or the person I'm left floating in the ocean with. Flying, it seems, is a gamble at every turn.

At last, I was secure in my tiny space. The plane hurtled down the runway, and I gripped my seat, hoping this wouldn't be the one making headlines tomorrow. I felt relieved when the shaking stopped, and the airport buildings shrank away, quickly becoming toy-like. However, my sense of calm was short-lived as the plane suddenly tilted at a ridiculous angle, before levelling out, only to encounter turbulence. This reminded me I had just strapped myself into a tin can now over 30,000 feet in the air. Normally a relaxed flyer, the extra emotion of the last few months heightened my anxiety. But I soon settled into the gentle hum of the plane, exploring the array of films available and negotiating the perfectly packed meal option.

It is only when I begin to relax after a stressful start to my trip that I think about why I'm here, where I'm going, and what I hope to achieve. The straightforward answers are:

- I've lost my partner of 44 years (married for 38), just three months after my dear mother passed away, and six months after we lost our beloved dog.

- I'm going to Australia to be with our pregnant daughter, and her family.

- I'm seeking solitude, but mainly peace, just peace.

This trilogy of loss, involving such different circumstances and relationships, brought about intense emotions and blurred lines that needed addressing before I could move on with my life. I was thoroughly exhausted, missing each of them terribly. I would stay up late, trying to be tired enough to sleep before unwanted thoughts kept me awake, which only worsened the situation.

Once Richard's cancer was deemed terminal, I knew I needed some sort of plan for life after his passing. When I mentioned this to a friend, she recommended that I read *The Salt Path*, a book about a couple setting off into the unknown of the South West Coast Path of England after losing everything.

Initially, it felt wrong to plan my single life by doing something we would have loved to do together. However, at that stage, it was a fantasy I could turn into a story and visualise. Every night, before unwelcome thoughts took over, I would force myself to imagine walking along the coast, meeting imaginary people, and looking out to sea.

I gained strength from picturing the sheer beauty of nature, where nobody knew me, and this trick helped me to sleep most nights. It also made the idea of travelling solo feel familiar. I'm not a natural hiker, so I knew the chances of walking for miles on end were slim, but it kept me focused on the unavoidable fact that one day I would be on my own and needed a plan to focus on.

Watching videos of people who had walked the 600 miles gave me confidence and a project to anticipate. Gradually, it didn't look so scary. I began to see that the future could hold excitement, and it also helped me numb my survivor's guilt. Raynor Winn, author of *The Salt Path*, explained at the start of her book that she didn't expect anyone outside of family would be interested in the details of their trip.

I felt similarly, unsure if anyone would care about my blisters and tears. However, many people insisted I keep them updated on my adventures, so I set up a social media group for sharing regular photos and messages. Not only was this a good way to inform them all at once about where I was, but it also generated incredible support and encouraging comments along the way. It helped me appreciate the thrill of following someone else's personal journey, brave the imposter syndrome, and gave me the courage to document my own experiences by writing everything down.

This trip felt like an escape, yet it was justified because

I already had a plane ticket, which had been changed numerous times for various reasons (originally planned with both of us going, but Richard's health intervened) and was too expensive to waste. Additionally, my daughter had asked if I could help with her toddler and newborn – a request that came at a time when I desperately needed a purpose in the aftermath of losing my husband and the ensuing emptiness.

My daughter had always been fiercely independent; she went backpacking at 18 and now, at 36, is happily married and settled far from home. Visiting her presented an opportunity for me to reset after the tumultuous past few years, to clear my mind of responsibilities, and confront my suppressed emotions and grief head-on. I needed to release my emotions freely, to scream into the wind and shout at the sea without anyone attempting to console me. Burying my feelings under distractions and pretending everything was fine would only deepen and intensify the ache in my heart, which I desperately wanted to ease.

Watching films and TV shows attentively about people walking through their grief, becoming mentally and physically stronger as they journeyed, resonated deeply with me. I wasn't a experienced hiker by any means, and a previous back injury added to the challenge, but the idea of escaping was appealing. Fortunately, early retirement and the sale of two cars had provided me with the means to embark on this journey – a chance to pave a path towards doing meaningful things for the remainder of my life.

Being at home proved problematic when I needed to physically react to my grief. There was always a well-meaning neighbour ringing the doorbell just when I wanted an ugly cry, or my son using his key to enter while I was still in bed at 4 p.m. The open windows and shared walls felt suffocating when I wanted to scream obscenities at the ceiling. Even walking my son's dog across the windy fields proved difficult, as other dog walkers would unexpectedly appear, leaving me too self-conscious to cry, or even talk to myself aloud.

There was no sea nearby to shout at, and I likely would have faced arrest if I had bellowed like an animal on Brighton beach. Yet, that was exactly the sort of release I craved. I yearned for space and solitude – somewhere I could immerse myself in the depths of my emotions and find a way to move forward.

June 2022…
Run away or stay?

…So, it looks like I'm going to be on my own soon. What happens to me then? I imagine myself going away, perhaps running away, my dog and I escaping all the tears and platitudes. We'd set off on a journey where no one would know me, just like in the books. Discovering unfamiliar places, meeting new people, being incredibly interesting, and finding the real, strong, and brave me while looking out to sea in bright, warm, and healing sunshine.

Or will I feel completely lost and lonely, in a strange place trying to prove to myself I can cope on my own, with no friends nearby? I will probably be wet and cold, trying to find somewhere to stay with a damp, smelly dog, both of us physically exhausted and just totally sad. What will I do?

It's a very romantic idea versus reality, when all I really want is to be safe at home where his presence will still surround me, and I can wallow in my loss and the life we shared together. Is there a right way? Two extremes with no real result. I guess I must take things slowly and do a bit of both, because it will not change anything as I am still going to feel incredibly sad and broken, so escaping grief is not really a healthy or likely option. I hope I will find the strength to let it happen naturally and wait patiently for time to heal, as I keep being told it will.

The advice to keep busy seems sensible, but it also sounds like a distraction from reality, and there are a lot of hours in the day to fill. I can't imagine it is very easy to be busy in the middle of a sleepless night. However, actively thinking and visualising myself making plans is preferable to waiting until it's too late and realising I have no clue what to do. It gives me a positivity for my future and distracts me from the present day. I think having any sort of plan is healthy and hopeful, as I am acutely aware that I will no doubt be reeling, and the tiniest piece of hope I can hold onto can only be good. I've stopped believing it will never happen; it will.

For now, I will just make the most of today.

My plan slowly took shape, and with the starting point sorted, I began to flesh out the rest. I would spend two months in Perth, Australia, to unwind with my daughter, let the dust settle, and welcome her new baby. I then intended to go on a solo six-week trip, heading towards the east coast of this immense continent – this would soon extend into a five-month adventure.

At this early stage, all I knew was that I wanted to follow the coast. I have a deep love for the sea and Australia boasted some breathtaking beaches. Previous visits had revealed the vast expanse of blue sky, the cinematic quality of the light, and the overall sense of well-being that came with the sun and warmth. Despite hearing my fair share of snake, spider, and shark stories, I wasn't one to be easily deterred. Seeking solace from this journey, I brushed off these anecdotes, refusing to let them trouble me.

Nearly everyone I spoke to offered a place to stay through a friend or family member, but I hesitated as I wasn't keen on imposing myself on others' hospitality. I didn't want to become the awkward guest leaving hosts uncertain of what to say or do. For the peace I craved, I was willing to risk occasional loneliness, preferring genuine solitude over constantly couch-surfing with my guard up.

Initially, my plan was simple; to hire a car from Adelaide to Brisbane and meander along the coastal road with the wind in my hair, feeling like a true adventurer. I envisioned stopping at friendly bed and breakfasts whenever the mood struck, without a care in the world. In Australia, they call people like that 'grey nomads' – carefree retirees spending their children's inheritance, celebrating their relationships, or embracing solo travel in campervans. I admired their freedom, although I never quite saw myself fitting that mould, and felt envious of their companionship. While I lacked a partner or a campervan, I still fit the brief and embodied the essence of being a retired traveller.

My uniform, consisting of three-quarter length, stretchy trousers, a pair of soft, yet sturdy shoes, a loose and easy-to-wash top, and a cardigan slung over my shoulders, seemed to confirm my status. And let's not forget the multi-pocket bag slung around my neck for safety, of course. It took some time to fully embrace this new identity, but the memory of sitting at the back of my first ferry ride on an early Monday morning, realising that we all looked the same, brought a smile to my face. Who would've thought it would be me?

After studying the cost of hiring a car for the entire trip, I opted to rely primarily on public transport instead. Renting a car would have amounted to thousands of pounds and introduced the stress of navigating unfamiliar roads, potentially distracting me from the scenic views.

The final plan involved an ambitious itinerary: 14 flights (8 domestic, 6 international), spanning 5 countries, 9 cities, 5 towns and 8 villages. I also planned for 4 coach trips, booked 2 hire cars, took 2 ferries, caught a couple of trains and taxis, and even included one bike ride – all within a period of five months.

March 2015…
Everest

…The onset of Richard's cancer sparked a genuine desire to become fitter both mentally and physically, prompting him to take on several walking and climbing challenges. Dog walking became a daily routine, and with open fields opposite our home, it turned into a very pleasurable activity, rather than a chore or necessary trip to retrieve the car from the pub. His early morning walks became his times for contemplation, with no one

around to witness his personal turmoil.

Suddenly, the idea of hiking up mountains became attractive, and he began to explore and undertake peak challenges whenever his health permitted. This pursuit added a great sense of purpose and accomplishment to his life. His daily walks became more goal-orientated, focusing on the number of steps taken, with encouraging voices from devices informing him exactly how far, how high, and how long he had walked. He would later recount these details to me with great enthusiasm. The varying degrees of the dog's exhaustion were usually my first indicator of the day's achievements.

A whole new determination emerged, leading to the purchase of various gear, with every possible outdoor trekking shop investigated. Beer money was now spent on weatherproof trousers and other equipment. This tremendously positive approach brought a fresh outlook to both our lives. It was inspiring to see how his passion for hiking and the great outdoors rekindled a sense of adventure and purpose.

It showed how doing new and challenging activities benefited everyone. It gave his supporters something positive to discuss, encourage, and donate towards – a tangible way of acknowledging the illness and actively contributing to his journey. This often led to people learning more about cancer and how it could be managed positively. It transformed the narrative from one of mere survival to one of thriving and hopefully inspired others to find their own ways to face adversity with courage and optimism.

I truly believe this defined Richard in the face of a terminal diagnosis, a fact our son, Michael, often pointed out. He surpassed the five-year mark given to him by the hospital, and fundraising became his passion, helping him achieve a certain peace of mind. He transformed from a potential grumpy old man into a man on a mission, determined to make the most of his time left and provide as much help as possible to others through the Royal Marsden Hospital. He set a humble example for all those around him, consequently making us very proud of his legacy. We agreed that any money raised after his death would go to the Royal Marsden, Banstead Cricket Club, and the Royal Alfred Seafarers' Society, where we both had worked for many years.

Everyone's personal mountain may not be as huge as Everest, but any constructive climb up the sheer rock face of cancer, while carefully negotiating loose rocks and slippery surfaces, can only be advantageous for all concerned. Richard's positive attitude influenced my trip tremendously and gave me the courage to take it on. How could I possibly sit at home dwelling when he had achieved so much in eight years?

The flight to Perth was smooth and uneventful. Although it was strange to leave my home, it wasn't as difficult as I thought, and gave me a real sense of purpose at last. My son Michael took me to Heathrow, and I felt excited to know I would soon be with my daughter. As always, arriving in Perth's heat was lovely, and I felt truly happy to be back in Australia. Knowing I could catch up with Catherine and share our emotions in no hurry this time, I settled in well and was pleased it was springtime and not the autumn I would be facing in England.

While awaiting the arrival of her new baby, I made the sensible decision to do a couple of dry runs of being alone by the sea to see what it felt like. Catherine dropped me off at their nearest beach, called Scarborough, where I stayed for two days and nights before catching the bus back to her house. I also decided to travel as light as possible, so this was also a packing test.

Taking what I considered essential, my backpack weighed 6.6 lb: four T-shirts, two pairs of shorts, one thin jumper, one pair of cropped trousers, one very lightweight jacket, leggings, a hoodie, underwear, an old shirt to sleep in, flip-flops, a wash bag with mini bottles of toiletries, an iPad, and a swimming costume. My reasoning was that I could wash things in basins with shampoo or soap, and they would dry overnight. Towels would be supplied, and if I got tired of the same clothes, I could buy more from a charity shop.

Wearing the heavier clothes and carrying just a small bag for my phone, I felt good. However, before my big solo trip, I decided to ditch the flip-flops. The shoes I wore could easily come off for the beach, and it wouldn't matter if they got wet and sandy. Every time I opened my pack, the flip-flops were in the way and rarely used. I also discarded one of the tops and the tatty thing I wore in bed, opting to wear one of the T-shirts instead. Small changes, but every ounce counted. I used my husband's bright orange rucksack, which he had taken on many hikes, so that felt right. And since I was never going too far from civilisation, I could buy anything I had forgotten along the way.

I walked down to the seafront, feeling strange being there alone. Miles of soft, white sand stretched in either direction, bordered by a sparkling sea with mighty waves. A few brave bodyboarders and kite surfers dotted the scene, but otherwise, it was empty.

This was my first foray into this unknown world, and as much as I embraced the view, I didn't know what to do with myself. I didn't know whether to turn left or right, sit down or stand up. Going anywhere seemed pointless without someone to share it with; eating out alone was heartbreaking, and drinking by myself was equally sad. I felt dreadfully lost and disoriented. I longed for my old life back, though I didn't feel homesick exactly, as I didn't want to be in my empty house. I desperately wished I could turn back time. After half an hour, I wandered back to my hotel room and felt sorry for myself until the evening.

Whenever we travelled as a couple, my husband made most of the daily decisions about where we went and what we did. I was very happy to follow his lead, having booked the flights and hotels. Suddenly, making even simple decisions floored me. Eventually, thirst and hunger made the choice for me, and I found a lovely fish restaurant on the beachfront. Bravely, I asked for a table for one, which seemed so alien to do. In true Australian style, I was welcomed warmly and given a table right in front of a beautiful sunset. I felt safe, comfortable, and extremely well-fed with a magnificent seafood platter.

The next day, feeling brighter, I decided to take a stroll along the sand, a wistful and thoughtful venture in true Brit style. I spotted the beachfront of the next town Cottesloe in the distance, 7 miles away (although it looked closer) and set off with flip-flops in hand, walking right along the water's edge. However, I quickly realised that expecting firm sand to walk on so close to the sea was wishful thinking. Making any forward progress became a mission as the sharp, shifting sand hurt my soft feet, and it felt like I was walking on glass! As if that wasn't enough, the tide was completely unpredictable. Initially, it appeared serene and tranquil, trickling up to gently lap at my toes. Yet, without warning, a huge wave surged forth, nearly taking me out, hitting me squarely side on at waist height. It became clear that this wouldn't be the journey I had anticipated. I retreated to continue on the pavement along the highway, determined to carry on.

Noting the absence of mad dogs, this Englishwoman continued her journey under the midday sun, firmly believing the next town was just around the corner. I had no water, no food, and no sunscreen – an embarrassing admission. I even refused to stop for brunch at a beach café, as I had found my rhythm and presumed there would be another one a little further on. Unfortunately, there wasn't. I was probably borderline delirious. The sun wasn't too bad, to be honest, but there was one spot on my left forearm that couldn't escape its rays, and after a while, I felt it burning. So, I took my arm out of the short sleeve and put it inside my top. Now, in addition to dragging my feet and being red in the face, I also appeared to have only one arm! I'm certain every passing motorist checked the news that night to see if the one-armed, red-faced, middle-aged lady had survived!

Eventually, feeling light-headed, I spotted a petrol station and thankfully purchased a bottle of water and a bar of chocolate. I sat on the edge of a wall until I regained some strength and, after acquiring directions, stumbled to a nearby train station to continue to my destination. After a brief, relaxing ride I still had to walk from the train station to the beach, and, by then, my legs were screaming. But I made it, only to discover that this seafront wasn't nearly as nice as the one I had left hours earlier. After two pints of water from a nearby pub, and feeling grateful for my Uber account, I travelled back to Scarborough and spent the rest of the day lying on my bed, staring at the ceiling, reflecting on my adventurous but exhausting day, until I finally fell asleep.

June 2022...
Jet

...I lost my beautiful boy, Jet, last week. He was my constant companion, and I had envisioned my future with him by my side once I was alone, after two anticipated losses. We were going to explore places he would enjoy, stay at special hotels that welcomed him warmly, and hike trails perfectly suited for a day's adventure. My bag would always carry his essentials before mine, his well-being taking priority, and we would do everything together. I would fill his ears with my inane chat, and he would hang on my every word. Having to put down my beautiful, black Labrador was heart-wrenching. He was only 8, and I was confident he would be there when I needed him most – licking away tears and wrapping his front legs around my neck, scratching me, but a pain worth bearing for such a comforting hug. Now, he won't be there to hear my woes, shoulder my emotions, or listen to my worries about the future, especially those I couldn't share with my husband.

A swift diagnosis of a severe problem left us with only an hour to decide, with the support of a compassionate vet. Since then, I have felt only relief, knowing he didn't suffer through a potentially painful ordeal.

My boy has left an enormous void. He may have been 'just a dog', but I loved him deeply and now that he's gone, my solitude feels even more profound. Dogs don't get funerals or a wake to help ease into grief; they simply vanish. Their beds and bowls are put away, and life is expected to resume immediately. There's no compassionate leave or grief counselling for their loss – just a sudden absence. Once the vacuum has removed the last of his hairs, that is it.

No more boy.

The second practice run was better. I booked a chalet on the beach on Rottnest Island for three nights. It's a small island about a 30-minute ferry ride from Fremantle, or an hour and a half from Perth quay, which included a beautiful boat ride down the Swan River. Rottnest is a lovely place, as there are no cars but many day trippers, who arrive in the morning and leave each evening on the returning ferry. Small, hopping, furry creatures called quokkas, about the size of a rabbit, harmless and quite cute, are a major selling point for the island, as they only live in Western Australia. I got a lot of pleasure from watching people being startled by them, often mistaking them for rats. But unlike the bloody flies, they were not a greedy nuisance and were a delightful tourist attraction.

For those seeking a longer break, chalets were available for rent, as were tents, either your own or in glamping sites, all conducive to the island's natural beauty and protected environment. This ensured it never felt overwhelmed with tourists. The island's history is poignant; it first served as a prison and later as a forced labour camp for Aboriginal people until 1931. Since 1993, the Rottnest Island Deaths Group Aboriginal Corporation has worked to raise awareness of this history, including the plight of the Aboriginal prisoners, the Quod (the old prison building), and the burial ground. Despite this dark past, the island has a gentle, respectful feel, making it a privilege to visit. It's undoubtedly one of my favourite places, with beautiful, secluded bays all around the coastline and smooth roads perfect for cycling.

My chalet was ideal once I arrived, following a hazardous bike ride. With time to kill before I could retrieve the key and unpack, I went to the pub and, after sinking two pints of cider, popped into the only food shop for three days' worth of supplies. Falling into the trap of believing I needed enough food for a family of five, I crammed it all into my backpack along with a bottle of red wine. In 35°C heat, I careered along the coastal path for 15 minutes on a hired bike with slipping gears and dodgy brakes, while a swarm of a thousand damned Australian flies seemed intent on invading my nostrils, eyes, and mouth, which I couldn't close as I was puffing too hard. My oversized helmet, grabbed hastily from the hire bin, slipped back almost choking me, but I didn't dare stop for fear of losing balance and shattering the wine, which would not only have been a dreadful waste but also a spectacle to behold.

The relief I felt upon opening the door to my chalet on my wobbly legs, spitting out flies, and laughing at myself, reminded me of my limits when travelling – I'm not cut out for too much discomfort. Both mini-breaks were teaching me valuable lessons, ones which made my poor daughter roll her eyes!

The view from my balcony encompassed a perfectly curved bay adorned with soft, white sand, and ample clear, turquoise, shallow waters, ideal for safe swimming. A few retirement boats bobbed in the distance, with creative names and sun-wrinkled occupants pondering their next moves. As the sunset painted the sky, I felt very peaceful with music playing from inside my chalet to keep me company. However, the emptiness around me was palpable, and once again, I strongly felt that something was missing. Yet, sitting on the balcony with such a breathtaking view also made me feel incredibly fortunate. Here, in these beautiful and tranquil surroundings, I was able to contemplate and face my grief. This was the first beach where I had found the quiet and solitude I craved. It affirmed my decision to embark on my solo journey in a few weeks' time. For the first time in a while, a small sense of excitement stirred within me, gently nudging the sadness aside.

The next day, I found a solitary café just a two-minute bike ride away, which served meals all day long. It may not have looked like much from the outside, but inside, the atmosphere was welcoming, the staff friendly, and it offered a convenient alternative to running the gauntlet of the fly-infested town centre. Taking a chance that evening, I was pleasantly surprised with the best fish curry I had ever tasted. The unassuming café also boasted home-made cakes, sandwiches, lovely coffee, and an off-licence. The following day's brunch was equally delightful, so I opted to stay near the chalet.

Overall, it was a lovely three-day break and just the right way to test myself before heading out on my own. Opting out of the initial car rental plan meant I had saved money and could appreciate nice, comfortable accommodation with scenic views. I realised how important this was in my search for peace and contentment. Crappy hotel rooms were not conducive to a good state of mind, as I would find out later.

These practice runs were my first true taste of solitude. The sound of the waves and the vast expanse of the sea provided a strange comfort, a reminder that the world is much larger than my personal grief. It gave me the confidence that I could manage longer journeys

alone and that my grief, while heavy, was something I could carry with me.

March 2015...
This doesn't happen to us

...We had passed the entrance and the signs to the famous Royal Marsden hospital numerous times, living just 3.3 miles away as we did. It was always where other people went so, I never dreamed how familiar those 3.3 miles would become.

I consider myself to be a reasonably strong person, able to process a situation, always looking towards a positive outcome. This wasn't even my own health issue so I thought accompanying my husband would be easy, a decent thing to do, just sitting and waiting, reading People's Friend, as he was led away down corridors that would become his second home.

However, I have never felt such a strong urge to turn and run away as I did when we first entered through the main doors into the foyer and the large waiting room.

I just didn't want to be part of this strange world of tired, brave people wearing bandanas or proudly bald, holding appointment cards with a knowing look on their face, waiting for their name to be called. We joined the people with hair and an anxious expression, no doubt feeling just the same disbelief and fear we did as we entered a surreal world of uncertainty, hope and camaraderie.

I see things very differently now; I feel nothing but compassion and pride for every single person in that waiting room and fierce gratitude for the way the staff treat all their patients equally.

I didn't attend my husband's appointments unless there was a serious update, I was just the chauffeur. It became his world, not mine. My interfering would have taken away the chance for him to take control of a situation he needed to master on his terms, dealing with his emotions directly instead of listening to my unnecessary opinion.

He met friends there and became on first name terms with the nurses, it became his life. He took in trays of cakes nearly every visit for the staff and fellow patients. He had a purpose and confidence in the challenge ahead.

I could not have been prouder of the way he strode into the hospital every single time for appointments, upright and brave, facing good news and bad news in equal measure with a protective smile to me on his return home, knowing of my discomfort of the situation.

Chapter 2

The Long Flight

Having safely welcomed my new grandson at the beginning of October (the date of which, would have been our 39th wedding anniversary) I set off on my solo trip on the 1st of November. It was springtime in Australia, an ideal season for comfortable travelling. I decided to fly from Perth to Adelaide to bypass the desolate Nullarbor Plain, a vast expanse of nothingness for miles on end. I had already booked to stay for four days on Kangaroo Island, a two-hour coach ride south of the city.

I stayed the night with a relative in Adelaide, took in some sights of the city, and enjoyed the beautiful beachfront. The next morning, I boarded the coach for a journey filled with bouncing, twisting turns, severe braking, uphill struggles, and a long downhill rush at the end, where I found myself praying the brakes would prevent us from plunging into the sea. Although the scenery was lovely, it was a bit of a white-knuckle ride.

Thankfully, the ferry trip that followed was smooth and short, and I arrived just a ten-minute walk from the seafront hotel I had booked for the first night. Once again, I was glad I had chosen not to rush things. I waited until early the following day to hire a car (as there is no public transport on the island), making it much easier to find my next chalet in the daylight.

Once I was on the road, I realised why it was called Kangaroo Island. It wasn't because I saw these lovely creatures happily bouncing around but rather due to the unfortunate amount of kangaroo roadkill scattered along the way, ranging from small to large and in various stages of decay. This was an unnerving sight, not just because any roadkill is distressing – whether badgers, pheasants, or foxes, as I was more accustomed to – but also because of the fear of accidentally colliding with one. In a small rental car, I had been warned about the senseless and unpredictable nature of kangaroos, often prone to leaping in front of vehicles. I couldn't shake the image of a potential accident, risking injury to either myself or a kangaroo in this remote area and possibly causing serious damage to the car.

Encountering wildlife is always expected in true countryside settings like this, but the prospect of hitting a kangaroo felt akin to hitting a deer in England, where at least I would know whom to call for assistance. Out here alone, it felt distinctly different and somewhat unsettling for the first leg of my journey.

Despite the sombre reality of roadkill, Kangaroo Island proved to be stunningly beautiful. On the way to my chalet, I stumbled upon an incredible, expansive beach, devoid of any other souls. During the hour-long drive, I encountered only two cars – an astonishingly quiet main road. The contrast between the bustling ferry and silent port added to a sense of isolation. It felt as though everyone had vanished, evoking a surreal sensation that perhaps I had missed some sort of apocalypse and was the sole survivor on the island. This feeling persisted as I explored further, often finding myself literally the only person for miles on end of pristine sand under the brilliant sunshine. Instead of dwelling on the mystery, I felt privileged to witness such untouched beauty and discover the places I had envisioned when planning my trip. My appreciation for the island deepened as I learnt about the devastating bushfires of 2020, the loss of both livestock and wildlife, and the ongoing efforts to restore and revitalize the island's ecosystem, as well as to reinvigorate tourism. Despite the challenges, Kangaroo Island remained a breathtaking destination, well deserving of a visit.

The chalet proved to be just like the photos on the website, though there was always the risk that requesting a sea view could result in needing to stand on a chair and squint over the top of bins to catch a glimpse of the ocean. Fortunately, my sweet accommodation exceeded expectations. Large windows adorned the front, positioned right next to my bed, framing a postcard-worthy view of five tall palm trees spaced perfectly to reveal the vast expanse of sparkling blue ocean just yards from my door, with the dappled headland in the distance.

I learnt that this very motel had suffered a massive blaze only months prior, resulting in the closure of the restaurant and some rooms. However, through tremendous dedication, it had been brought up to an excellent standard. I felt a sense of satisfaction knowing I had supported them in some small way. Once again, I seemed to be the sole guest. I opened the net curtains as wide as possible and lay on the bed, soaking in the view for what felt like ages.

In the early evening, four large pelicans flew right across my view, circled, and flew slowly past again – a scene reminiscent of *Jurassic Park*.

Eventually, I ventured towards civilization in search

of food. This time, I stumbled upon a large, historic hotel with a huge bar and dining room decorated with pictures of local characters and history. While the dates might have been relatively recent compared to those in London, they were nonetheless well-recorded with evident pride in their past. The food was perfect, though the obligatory air conditioning proved a nuisance. I found myself eating quickly to prevent it from chilling my meal too soon. While I appreciated the comfort of air conditioning, when necessary, I couldn't help but long for a respite from the wind outside, especially as I was only wearing a light coat at this stage.

Again, the view from my table was enviable, and I knew I would enjoy the next few days. On my way back, I stopped at an off license and encountered a short, weathered man behind the counter. When I asked for a bag, he responded with 'We don't do bags, but a box will do you right, as the last thing I need is you dropping your wine and then expecting me to find you a straw so you can run to the bottom

of the hill and suck it up before it reaches the drain'. It was a fantastic, droll, and long-winded response! Imagine a thick, resigned Australian accent with every third word an expletive, and you'll understand why I laughed all the way back to the chalet.

On the second day, I drove to Seal Bay in the south of the island. As the name suggests, it is a haven for sea lions and is simply stunning. Here, I finally encountered other tourists and realised I preferred the solitude of my earlier explorations. The crowds seemed to rush through these beauty spots, snapping photos, making quick stops at the souvenir stands and toilets, before hurrying back to their coaches.

I've always been a reluctant tourist, favouring to seek out my own entertainment rather than following the herd, but I understand that these places rely on the influx of visitors. The setup at Seal Bay was impressive, with a long walkway leading to a lookout over the dunes and beach, where sea lions were guaranteed to appear. Lounging about and wading into the surf, they are truly magnificent creatures, and seeing them in their natural habitat was a highlight of my visit.

On the 4th of November, back in England, my village held its annual firework display, celebrating Guy Fawkes Day which lands on the 5th. My husband and I had run this event for the past 40 years, and now it was being organised by our son, which would be attended by thousands of locals. This year was particularly special, as after the main event, a short display of six magnificent rockets would send some of Richard's ashes high into the sky – a wish he had expressed since the day I met him.

With the significant time difference, I watched this beautiful spectacle at six in the morning, live on my phone, as the sun rose over my sea view. Tears streamed down my face, but they were tears of pure joy. We had fulfilled his wishes, and this left me with a cherished memory of Kangaroo Island that will stay with me forever.

The day before my departure, two new guests moved into the chalet next to mine. Their surprise was evident as they passed by and caught me lounging on my bed which was pressed up against the window, resembling one of those ladies in Amsterdam – although I was fully clothed, devouring a bar of chocolate, and nursing a glass of red wine!

Leaving Kangaroo Island was bittersweet. Despite my reluctance to bid farewell, a hectic day of travelling lay ahead. I set off at 6 a.m. with the aim to return the car to the ferry port by 8 a.m. The lady working for the car rental company had warned me about the active kangaroos during that time, so I drove cautiously. I tucked in and trailed behind the only lorry in sight, hoping its presence would deter any curious marsupials from venturing onto the road. Thankfully, the journey to the ferry was uneventful. After the brief crossing, I boarded the return coach to Adelaide, bracing myself for another nerve-wracking ride, albeit with a different driver.

Several hours later, I boarded a flight bound for Hobart, Tasmania. Upon arrival, I hopped on an airport shuttle bus that whisked me away to my hotel near the waterfront.

Proud of my meticulous travel arrangements thus far, I was swiftly brought back to reality upon entering the hotel room I had booked for the next six nights. I won't mention the establishment by name as it wasn't the fault of the company, but rather my own choice – or perhaps the exorbitant price tag attached to a room boasting a picturesque, unobstructed view over the waterfront, which would have been three times what I had paid.

The room itself was impeccably clean and adequately comfortable, yet it lacked character. A narrow, fixed window at the end of the room gave it a prison-like atmosphere. Situated five stories up, with my nose pressed against the glass, the view was disappointingly mundane and offered little more than a glimpse of the rear of a bar and a block of offices, with only a sliver of sky and sea visible. Admittedly, this outlook was par for the course for most of the rooms, primarily intended for corporate or overnight stays. There were moments when I longed to retreat to my room, and the accommodation did little to lift my spirits. Fortunately, Hobart proved to be a charming town with a captivating waterfront and several things to see and do.

It dawned on me just how crucial a great view and an openable window were to my sense of well-being. Instantly, the room's lacklustre ambiance made me feel isolated and melancholic, prompting me to spend more time outdoors. I stacked the pillows beside me, imagining my husband's comforting presence in the darkness – a practice I hadn't resorted to since the initial weeks after his passing.

May 2023…
Bored of being alone

…I wake up, and it's just me. I go to bed, and it's still just me. Watching TV alone has its moments – the joy of controlling the remote and not enduring cricket – but it's short lived, because it's still just me. I eat whatever I want, if I can be bothered, without anyone else offering an opinion or needing feeding. Sometimes I find myself talking to myself or to your photo because there's no one else to listen.

I don't always feel lonely, but I am bored with my own company without casual conversation, laughter, or the back-and-forth of plans, discussions or even arguments. I crave sharing my day, my ideas and silences or cuddles with someone who knows me, with whom I have shared a history and a future.

Our inside jokes fall flat, our secret, knowing looks or raised eyebrows are no longer shared. I'm tired of being alone. I never realised how much I would miss someone I could truly be myself with, an irreplaceable trust formed over years of companionship.

No one to make a cup of tea for, to order a curry with, or to judge my choice of clothes with impatient platitudes. No one to nag about abandoned dinner plates or work boots left in the wrong place. No one to ask, for the hundredth time, to get their sports kit out of the car so it can be washed. I can't laugh at you being defeated by the car park payment app or endure your huff because you forgot your watch yet again, blaming me for some reason.

No more leaving the house together, shouting requests and commands at each other, checking who has locked the back door, let the dog out, left a light on, got money, or the directions to a venue. Doing anything is just not fun anymore, it feels lifeless and meaningless when it isn't shared. I'm told I'm making new memories, but they feel shallow when they exist only in my head.

It's the silly things that make a relationship – the years of the same person in my face, watching their reactions to my words, and getting that little jump in my heart when I see the familiar big smile emerge after a shared memory, taking us back to being teenagers again.

I miss that person so desperately now – the physical body to grab for a squeeze or a tease, the smile that reassured me that life is okay even when I moaned about trivial stuff. The annoying person in front of the fridge or in the bathroom at precisely the same time I needed to be there. The person I could love or hate within seconds, and the warm body I shared my bed with, making the world alright again with quiet pillow talk, preparing for the next day.

The hole in my heart is ever-present and I don't really know how to fill it. All I know is I miss the very essence of you. I miss the strength of your awkward arm around me in bed, the prickle of your stubble when you kissed me, and your snore when I thought you were listening to my woes. I miss your honesty about not wanting to die, as you still had so much to do, seeing that frustration and regret in your eyes. I miss your strength and bravery.

I can't change any of this. I miss you being in the way. Damn, I miss you.

Minimising my time in the hotel room, I set out to explore the city. I avoided the main shopping areas, as I consider shops to be largely uniform worldwide. Instead, I took a bus tour to get my bearings, visited the maritime museum, and strolled through the historic quarters that housed artisan craft shops and galleries showcasing Aboriginal art. Along the waterfront, I indulged in people-watching, soaking in the panoramic views and the serene expanse of sky and sea.

I enjoyed some lovely meals, though the portions were often oversized. Even the salads were enormous, and I longed for something lighter. As a result, I often brought leftovers back to my room.

A week before leaving England, I cracked a tooth, and despite having it addressed the day before departure, it continued to bother me. I had to be cautious, and everything I ate or drank had to be taken into consideration. A fresh juicy watermelon or orange would have made me jump out of my skin, and cereal was crunchy and soaked in cold milk, even smoothies posed a challenge. I resolved to locate an emergency dentist at some point.

The juxtaposition between old and new buildings, in the capital, was fascinating, and the pride in their history, particularly naval, was evident everywhere. Flying into Hobart offered a striking view over mountains and lush grasslands, a stark departure from the flatter, drier Australia I had observed earlier in the flight. Tasmania seemed akin to New Zealand, a similarity I would soon confirm firsthand in a few weeks. The weather in Hobart was warm and sunny during my visit, although I was aware it could turn cold and wet here. Fortunately, my backpacking gear proved adequate, and I only needed to use my lightweight jacket on a couple of occasions.

I visited the MONA (Museum of Old and New Art) across the harbour, courtesy of their special boat. It was an amazing, interactive place, a haven for true art lovers, with so much to see – very modern and delightfully eccentric. Although it wasn't entirely my cup of tea, witnessing the obvious effort that had gone into it was fantastic. The tremendous attention to detail was remarkable, and the museum, constructed across four underground levels, even featured a bar built into the rock. It stood out from other museums and was definitely worth experiencing.

I loved its position on the River Derwent, with its stunning views, and the friendly and relaxed atmosphere of the outdoor space. It was easy to spend hours there, sipping a drink in the shade after emerging from the depths of the exhibits. The boat trip alone provided a great perspective on the entire Hobart area, so I didn't feel the need to take a separate tourist trip around the harbour during my stay.

The next day, I visited the famous Saturday Salamanca Market in the old part of town. There were hundreds of interesting stalls with local produce and handmade goods. The scallop skewers were absolutely delicious! Something I had never seen before and I could have eaten several more.

Of course, I made the rookie mistake of finding perfect gifts to take back home too early in my trip. However, they were ideal and different from the typical airport or city gift shops: local, lightweight items. That was until I realized I needed 30 gifts, which meant 30 lightweight things added up to one heavy thing. I intended to post them back to Perth, but since I wasn't hiking miles, I just put up with the extra baggage in my backpack.

I succumbed to a glass of wine after the market and sat at a big, empty table. Soon, a group of lads, clearly on a Saturday afternoon session, approached and asked if they could sit down. I agreed and even offered to move, as they mentioned more of their friends were on the way. However, with much gesturing and many expletives (followed by apologetic expletives for the expletives), they included me in such a friendly and typically Australian way.

It was evident they were in for a long drinking session, but once they saw I didn't mind their rowdy manner, it was nice to be the centre of attention for half an hour. They didn't stop ribbing each other, and I couldn't imagine what twelve hours hence would bring. With my sports club and horse racing background, I was able to hold my own. When they all wished me well and moved on to the next bar, I had a big smile on my face. I was flushed not only from the wine but from the presence of the locals having fun and the joy of seeing a bit of life again after so much solitude. The table next to me was full of the beige stretch trouser and cardigan brigade, a stark contrast to the lively company I had just enjoyed!

The next day, I had some time to kill between checking out of the hotel and catching a coach to go up the west coast. I found a pleasant square with cafés and shops where I could sit in the sun and pass the time. The area was relatively quiet, but I noticed a few people were leaving with their hands over their children's ears. Curious, I soon discovered the reason: a group of young men were in an outside bar, laughing and swearing loudly after an early Friday release from work. Their voices echoed around the small square, making it quite unpleasant and disrupting the otherwise peaceful ambiance.

This scenario was not as comfortable as the previous day at the market, so I decided to find somewhere else to spend my time. I spotted an old bookshop and ducked inside. It was lovely and quiet, until the door opened, and the shop was momentarily filled with expletives from the rowdy group outside. The customers shuddered until the door's slow-close mechanism finally kicked in, allowing peace to be restored.

Now, I may or may not have gone into this shop,

but it proved to be a turning point in my trip. There, I immediately spotted the third book in *The Salt Path* trilogy. Having loved the first two, I couldn't resist purchasing it. I spent the following few hours immersed in its pages along the waterfront, feeling deeply inspired to start penning my own story.

While waiting for the coach, I noticed a familiar face from the MONA ticket office. She approached me, recognising the book, and we struck up a lovely conversation which lasted for a good fifteen minutes. She shared her fondness for the series and mentioned she intended to buy the third book also. We exchanged stories of our travels and future plans before she wished me well and went on her way, leaving me with a real sense of connection.

Determined to complete the book by the time I returned to Hobart, which I did, I carried it with me to the closed ticket office. There, I left it with a note for the tall, friendly lady who checked people's tickets, squeezing it through the shutter, with hopeful anticipation she would get it. I signed my name at the bottom of the note, leaving no other details. Perhaps one day, she will come across my name in a bookshop and recognise herself in the story!

August 2021...
Please listen to me

...I feel like I have already lost you. You are not talking to me except to say, 'I'm fine'. Whenever you say that, I know you're not. If you say it lightly, then I know you're just not good; if you say it firmly with hard eyes, I know you're really not good, and that further questions are not welcome. A full stop between us.

You're just coping, don't want to talk, need to process and withdraw until the feeling passes, leaving me in the dark, not knowing what on earth you are thinking.

Well, as it happens, I am not fine either. I'm stuck in

the middle, wondering how you are feeling and what I could do to help. I want to know everything you are thinking because I need the chance to help in some small way, and I would love to discuss your feelings and be a good wife. But all you give me is 'fine'. I'm doing my very best to understand, but please help me out. I thought we were in this together.

I find out more from your friends and colleagues whom you have spoken to. They get a better answer than I do, and that hurts me. I don't even think you are protecting me; I'm honestly not sure what's going on, but I feel offended that you think I will either make a big deal of it or get all emotional and cry. Then you don't know me at all. I'm here for you; please let me in.

I bite my tongue yet again, and although I feel so proud of how you are dealing with this situation, I still feel really left out. I'm sure I would have healing words if I was given the chance, but probably, deep down, I'm also afraid of opening that emotional door.

I know you are.

Suppressing all our emotions is par for the course, sadly. You always say there is nothing to talk about as it is all ifs, buts, and maybes. You said right at the beginning that we will talk about it when there is something to talk about, apparently. That may protect you from the reality, but I need to talk, waffle on, hear our voices mingled together, just airing and sharing. It doesn't have to be deep, and our thoughts may change next week, but let's talk together while we can.

I've joked I'll put the words 'I'm fine' on your gravestone and that you will save all the important, serious stuff for your deathbed, but we may never even get that privilege. Until then, I've learnt to respond with a resigned smile, laugh about it, and move on again, closing my own emotional doors.

The three-hour coach trip up the east coast to a quiet place called Bicheno proved to be yet another full-body workout. Every bend tested my legs and core strength, and even my backpack needed its own safety belt! Frustratingly, I discovered that despite assurances from the visitor centre that the coach would accept cards, however, the driver insisted on cash. The stroppy man was reluctant to let me on, I offered to ring the company and pay by phone, which he begrudgingly allowed. I didn't trust him not to kick me off early if that didn't work. My phone wouldn't connect to the internet, but fortunately I managed to ring my daughter, who was able to make the payment for me. At the end of the journey, the driver smugly informed me that he knew I had paid because he had checked.

The coach journey provided glimpses of beautiful views from the window, although my attention was divided between them and my music playlist through earphones, trying to avoid the discomfort of the rough ride. Rushing past a sign that read 'BreakMeNeck Hill' only added to the nerves. I had chosen Bicheno somewhat randomly based on its promise to offer a private, secluded, and detached chalet right by the beach with an ocean view. On paper it seemed simple and tranquil – just what I craved at the time.

Having not heard from the host since I booked, I decided to give him a call. To my surprise, I learnt that the chalet was five miles from the bus stop in town. It was a Sunday afternoon when I was due to arrive, and there were no taxis in the area. The owner, embodying the typical Australian kindness, generously offered to pick me up that evening. His hospitality was a comforting reminder of the warmth and friendliness I had encountered throughout my travels.

Standing there, watching the coach disappear was a bit daunting. The town seemed utterly still, with everything closed and no houses nearby. I hoped my landlord would come and rescue this stranded middle-aged lady with the orange backpack soon. Yet, right on the dot of the arranged time – or rather, the time he said, 'You'll be 'right, no worries' – a solitary pickup truck turned the corner. We introduced ourselves, and I gladly accepted the offer to throw my pack into the back of his truck.

Seeing my chalet was pure joy; I absolutely loved it. I knew this would be a game-changer, and I was right. The raised unit featured an open-plan, spacious layout: a full kitchen, a huge bed and bathroom, laundry facilities, a lounge and dining area. The attention to detail was excellent, right down to the quality tissues and toilet rolls. This was all complemented by a long balcony with the promised ocean view just beyond the dunes and bushes. I could hear the waves crashing, and the vast sky above was deep, comforting blue. Immediately, I felt safe and at ease.

Again, the food issue came up as I had only managed to fit four bananas and three chocolate bars into my pack. However, I knew there would be a welcome hamper waiting for me, so I planned to make do. My host had kindly invited me to go to

the supermarket the next day, but to be honest, I didn't want to leave the chalet for a second, especially for mundane tasks like grocery shopping.

The hamper turned out to be very generous, with home-made bread, jam, and butter, their own eggs, milk, cheese, and cream. Two large jars of locally sourced granola and a mini bar topped it off. I asked if I could buy some extra eggs from them instead of going shopping and hunkered down with what I had for the next few days. The bounty of local, home-made goods allowed me to fully enjoy my secluded retreat without venturing out for supplies.

After having scrambled eggs on toast for dinner, I lit the wood burner to stave off the evening chill, opened a bottle of local wine, and sank into the comfy sofa while gazing at the view and listening to the waves. It was then that I silently cried. I cried for my loss, I cried with relief that the intense period of grief was finally easing, and I cried simply because I needed to. Here, in the solitude of my chalet, I felt certain of no interruptions, allowing me to release my emotions freely.

These tears weren't the loud, uncontrollable sobs of the early days; rather, they were tears of pure grief that flowed throughout most of the evening. I found myself reflecting heavily on my mum, who had passed away just three months before my husband. During his illness, I had to push aside my grief for her, but now, in this tranquil setting, memories of her came rushing back. It had been a year marked by loss, including my beloved dog early on, and I felt deeply overwhelmed by the weight of death. As the tears continued to flow, I let myself mourn these significant losses, allowing myself to reach an emotional depth that I had suppressed.

Over the next few days, I felt a welcomed personal shift within myself. Perhaps it was due to finally settling into my solo trip, or maybe it was the peaceful surroundings of this place that I had envisioned for so long.

July 2023...
The good, the bad and the ugly

...There are three distinct types of day when you are grieving.

Type 1: *You wake with a deep, heavy weight at your core. Tears hover just beneath the surface all day, and you sense that even the smallest trigger could bring you to tears or leave you holding your head in your hands, convinced this is your new normal.*

Type 2: *You leap out of bed, full of plans. You're determined to clear out belongings, wipe the slate clean, and move forward with confidence and joy. You almost convince yourself that you're finally done with grief.*

Type 3: *The day moves in slow motion. You feel neither particularly happy nor sad, but wear an easy smile on your face. You're mostly content, accepting, a bit nostalgic, and calm. You're kind to everyone, just* *drifting through the day.*

I haven't yet figured out the patterns behind these types yet. Sometimes, my dreams from the night before shape the day ahead. Dreaming about him leads to a Type 2 day, while a bit too much wine the evening before often results in a Type 1 day – my own fault and something I'm addressing!

The Type 3 day remains a mystery. Today was one of those days, and surprisingly, I found myself being my nicest self – engaging in gentle conversations with strangers, feeling no frustration with others, and even gifting a huge bar of chocolate to the petrol station attendant just because he made me smile.

So, here's something else no one tells you: you never know what to expect. Let it unfold naturally, embrace the good moments, endure the tough ones, and above all, be kind to yourself.

Waking up to a beautiful day in the most comfortable

bed I had ever slept in, I decided to have fried eggs on toast for breakfast, bypassing the granola due to my tooth. After a refreshing shower, I treated myself by putting six items of clothing into the washing machine – a small luxury compared to hand-washing. I then took a short walk to the beach, just 30 seconds away. Once again, I was greeted by miles of pristine sand and the wide-open sea. The water, seemingly calm, would occasionally form last-minute waves that resembled those in an oil painting, gently rolling towards the shore to touch my bare feet. Apart from seagulls and the occasional crab, I had this paradise all to myself. The brilliant sunlight illuminated the entire scene like a perfectly staged film set.

Emotionally drained from the previous evening, I found myself crying again, but this time the tears were different – they were tears of happiness, acceptance, and hope. I felt a deep sense of gratitude for being able to confront my grief head-on in this place, as I had wished. I felt incredibly fortunate. As I wrote Richard's name in the sand, a ritual I had also performed at Rottnest, I realised I didn't need to shout at the sea as I had once thought. My path had shifted significantly, and I sensed the beginnings of recovery. Perhaps most surprisingly, the heavy ache in my chest, the physical pain that had weighed me down, had begun to ease. To mark this moment, I boiled a couple of eggs as a snack – a simple act of celebration amidst the profound emotions I was experiencing.

My desire to write blossomed during those three days in Bicheno. It provided me with complete freedom to simply be myself, unencumbered by responsibilities or constraints. After enjoying yet another omelette, I immersed myself in reading my new book and working on my own writing. I even managed to squeeze in a nap and returned to the beach twice more that first day, revelling in the knowledge that I had two more days ahead to write and soak in the sea before returning to Hobart. After scrambling three eggs for dinner, I slept deeply and peacefully, feeling content.

The following day unfolded much the same, though

I made an effort to nibble on some granola and enjoy bread, jam, and cheese. On my last morning in Bicheno, I finished off the eggs and my final banana, packed up my backpack, ensured the chalet was left in pristine condition, and reluctantly bid farewell. True to his word, my landlord kindly gave me a lift back to catch the only coach of the day. Reflecting on it now, I believe Bicheno may have been the most memorable place of my entire trip – its location, the timing of my visit, and the profound emotional changes it brought about in me.

I had never anticipated where or how different emotions would manifest, if at all, but after my time in Bicheno, I became acutely aware of the potential to reconnect with myself and envision a future when I least expected it. This journey through grief has taught me the importance of maintaining an open mind and an open heart, allowing for unexpected moments of healing and growth.

I was now ready for the return coach trip and

arrived safely back in Hobart, where I checked into a different hotel on the waterfront for my final night. To my delight, I received an upgrade which gave me a lovely view across the wide river. Even better, the room had windows that could be opened, allowing the fresh Tasmanian air to fill the space. It was a fitting end to my journey, enjoying the sights and sounds of the evening wanderers. As I reflected on my time in Tasmania, I knew deep down that I would return.

The bus ride to Hobart airport the next morning and the flight to Melbourne were both uneventful, and upon arrival, I was greeted by an old friend. It was wonderful to see someone from home, and we spent two days catching up. After that, I moved to an apartment hotel on Brighton Beach. This was my third Brighton experience since arriving, and it was beautiful with its backdrop of the city and a fair number of people around, a change from the quieter spots I had been in. There weren't any shops nearby, but luckily, the yacht club was directly opposite, offering a place for evening meals and Sunday lunch.

In typical Australian fashion, it was casual rather than posh.

I had secured a room with a balcony, which was perfect. It allowed me to enjoy sitting in the sun, listening to music, and continuing to write. This accommodation was not only good value for money, but also crucial for feeling comfortable, especially during these times. I had no desire to rush around visiting cities or doing obligatory sightseeing. Instead, I found solace in peace, quiet, and a scenic view, which was truly nourishing for my soul.

Unfortunately, my toothache suddenly worsened overnight, and I had used up the emergency painkillers I had with me. I was eager to get to the airport in hopes of buying more, as I wasn't sure I could manage until I got home. The flight to Newcastle, north of Sydney, was smooth, and I had the pleasure of sitting next to a very interesting lady who shared some fascinating stories. Travelling alone allowed me to meet many people in passing, which was a nice change, though

I quickly learnt not to divulge too much too soon, as well meaning do-gooders always seemed ready with their solutions to everything!

Upon arrival at the airport, I had an amusing encounter during customs. Following an X-ray, I was frisked by a young man who seemed unsure about something on his screen. After an awkward ten minutes, his female colleague came over and quickly resolved the issue: the *'suspicious lump'* under my left arm wasn't a bag of drugs but my left boob, in holiday mode, unsupported within a comfortable bra! She chuckled knowingly while the young man avoided eye contact as I walked away, smiling at the humorous misunderstanding. Poor boy!

I was warmly greeted at the airport by family members, and spent two days being pampered with all the comforts of home. They showed me around Newcastle, a city with a fascinating harbour, picturesque cliffs, and beautiful beaches. The historic port, once celebrated for its extensive coal export industry, now intrigued me with its juxtaposition against a massive storage area filled with thousands of old wind turbine blades.

After enjoying freshly washed clothes and a hearty meal, I picked up a rental car for the next leg of my coastal journey. Driving three hours north, I reached Port Macquarie on the east coast, where I intended to spend five nights exploring and relaxing.

I was surprised by the lack of convenient public transport options up the coast, so I decided to hire a car for this leg of the journey. My daughter and I had searched, but the only bus left at 9:30 p.m. meaning it would arrive at 3:30 a.m. This would be useless for me, as I wasn't keen on finding my chalet in the middle of the night. Driving again was a pleasant change though, especially in a comfortable hybrid car, making my journey up the Pacific Highway highly enjoyable. The landscape along the coastline, with its greenery and rolling hills, gradually changed as I headed further north. It felt grounding to be on the road instead of flying and driving up the east coast of Australia was an exhilarating experience for me.

Having a car also proved to be useful in my hunt for a dentist and for everyday tasks. I had developed a small blister on my heels after a short, hot walk to the shop without socks, so the car was a godsend on many levels. Driving in Australia is a delight; they drive on the familiar left side of the road, and the roads are wide, well-maintained, and less congested compared to England. People seem more relaxed, and finding parking is generally easy. Additionally, the regular and well-kept rest stops along the way were appreciated during the journey.

I settled into the three-bedroom town house quite easily and immediately felt comfortable. Spread across three levels, it offered everything I could wish for, including a garage, three balconies/decks, and a large garden area that provided a different atmosphere from the usual sea view. Although the ocean was just a short five-minute walk away, it was refreshing to encounter kookaburras, large lizards, and bush turkeys up close. The lush surrounding trees added to the charm and beauty of the place.

One friendly neighbour, after a rather probing conversation, suggested that my ever-present kookaburra might be a sign of my husband looking after me. While I am open-minded and appreciated the sentiment, I suspected that the leftover chips I had accidentally dropped on the balcony were more likely the reason why this beautiful bird frequented my area! This wise animal seemed to have spread the word that I was a sloppy eater among its friends, as I woke up to a small zoo outside my window every morning thereafter. The cacophony of numerous kookaburras at 5 a.m. was like a hundred monkeys arguing, serving as my unexpected alarm clock.

Keen to return to solitude after some enforced

socialising, I reverted back to the traveller's diet of eggs, chocolate, cheese, bananas, bread, and jam. I limited myself to one shop visit because I didn't want to waste time on boring, domestic tasks. It became somewhat fun to embrace minimalist eating. Each place I stayed provided a decent coffee machine with milk and often biscuits, so anything I purchased had to be the right size to consume quickly or be nonperishable enough to carry with me to the next destination. As a result, I skipped buying items such as butter or milk. Chocolate and bananas became a decent alternative and reliable backup. Even if the chocolate melted, it hopefully wouldn't leak.

Annoyingly, the shop only offered a pack of 100 plasters for my single blister, which was a shame but necessary. The lone emergency plaster I had packed proved useless as it had lost its adhesive after being shuffled through multiple bags over time. Moreover, the dusty mints buried at the bottom of the same bag had welded to the lining, prompting me to reluctantly buy a new tin. The spare contact lenses I carried for emergencies were outdated and although they weren't ideal, they were better than having none at all. My fresh lenses were safely packed in my main suitcase, which was back in Perth.

After just over three weeks in, I took stock of my luggage and found that, aside from my early gift-buying mistake in Hobart, everything was working out quite well. The only items I hadn't used yet were my swimming costume and leggings, as my three-quarter length trousers were sufficient for most occasions. I had even worn my nice top on an evening out. Knowing my next hotel had a pool; I was sure I'd get to use the swimsuit soon.

Both my coat and hoodie had come in handy, and I had become an expert at washing clothing in a sink, making two sets of underwear sufficient. I bought a notepad because I still preferred to write some things by hand, but otherwise, I didn't feel I had made any major packing mistakes. As I was becoming accustomed to living on my own, this suited me, and repacking was a breeze since I had minimal waste. I had removed painkillers and plasters from their bulky boxes and kept a couple of hotel shampoos and soaps handy, which also doubled for washing clothes.

Aside from the gifts for home, I had collected a few special shells and stones with memories attached, as well as handwritten notes detailing my travel plans to organise later. While it was tempting to keep maps, guides, and boarding passes, I realised they wouldn't hold much meaning for anyone else back home, so I disposed of them. Each time I flew, I relished the simplicity of managing just one backpack without the hassle of claiming or struggling with a large suitcase.

The favourable weather and staying in accommodations with basic amenities meant I didn't need to pack towels or bedding, which further streamlined my experience.

Knowing it was my final week of solitude before joining family in New Zealand, I fully embraced it and allowed myself to confront my loss head-on. I deliberately immersed myself in memories, looking at photos and recalling moments, which made me cry easily. I watched the video of his memorial, closed all the windows, and played music loudly, drowning out the noise of the ceiling fans which were on full blast. Doing this brought some relief and reinforced the idea that grief needs to be acknowledged and processed. Even if I felt I was drowning at times, I never doubted that I would resurface eventually, drawing deep lungfuls of pure, fresh air to sustain me for the future. The ugly, gut-wrenching grief had lessened and, even though the tears still came regularly, it was getting easier overall.

After that emotional release and another omelette, I felt back on course and headed to the beach. I found a picture postcard place of natural beauty where I sat for half an hour, soaking in the scenery. Unfortunately, my throbbing tooth forced me to return to the house for a painkiller. The day before, I had tried diligently to secure an emergency dental appointment, but it proved impossible, despite what their websites stated. Faced with the uncertainty of getting major dental work done far from familiar surroundings, I decided to manage with painkillers until I could be with family again. I stretched out the intervals between tablets longer than recommended, hoping it would be okay.

By the last day of my stay in Port Macquarie, I felt ready to move on. The house had been comfortable, with plenty of light, but I missed the direct views of the sea. While the garden had been a pleasant change, it was really the expansive sky that lifted my spirits, so I was eager to get back into my hire car and head to my next destination.

I left at 5 a.m. to save on rental costs by returning the car to Ballina before 10 a.m., though it made for a long day. Typically, I welcomed staying in bed late, as it's difficult to grieve whilst unconscious.

November 2023…

Cotton wool horizon

…I am not brave, nor am I strong. All I'm doing is coping with a situation I had no control over. It's been 30 weeks today since I lost my husband – 7 and a half months, or 210 days if you like.

Initially, family brought me to Australia, and now cowardice keeps me here longer, tied to the duration of a special visa that will eventually send me home to face my new life. I was content with the old one, and the word 'new' sounds like everything will be fresh and shiny, but I doubt that.

People tell me I'm making memories. No, I'm not. Memories are shared with others so you can revisit them years later, exchanging knowing smiles that speak volumes without needing words. My travels consist of seeing places through my eyes alone. Australia is undeniably beautiful, and I'm grateful for the opportunity. I have no regrets about how things ended, and I'll resist the temptation to manufacture any now – it would only be self-torture.

Motivation eludes me; everything seems pointless. I recognise how having companionship and conversation helps reveal inner feelings. A sounding board, saying things out loud, often answers your own questions and quells the doubts created in silence, spurring creativity. I'm also bloody sick of eating alone.

I know I'll grow braver and stronger. This feeling isn't enjoyable; it's just a tough day in the midst of what should be a great adventure. It's a necessary trough, and I'll take my time as it passes. One thing is certain: resisting or distracting myself won't work; This wave of emotion will return until it feels acknowledged.

This is my cotton wool horizon, viewed from the aeroplane window, as mentioned previously – clouds that appear as solid as mountains until you reach out to touch them, only to find them dissolve into mist. That's how elusive my future feels right now.

The drive up the Pacific Highway was lovely, especially in its later stretches, though it's more of a highway than a true coastal road, albeit running parallel to the coastline. I saw a beautiful sunrise, with thick layers of mist across the fields and the morning light hit the sides of the hills in spectacular fashion. Despite it being a Monday morning, I only encountered real traffic in Coffs Harbour, as the highway cuts right through the middle of the town.

During the drive, I kept a wary eye on my petrol gauge, which was dropping faster than expected. I was required to refill the tank before returning the car, so wanted to leave it as late as possible. Though I had passed several service areas earlier, they seemed to disappear when I needed them most. Converting kilometres to miles didn't help my guesswork either. Just as my nerves were setting in, I finally found a service station, filled up, and hurried towards Ballina.

My timing was a tad off, and I rushed the last bit, desperately trying to find the car drop-off before the deadline. Deep in the middle of a huge industrial estate, the map directions on my phone proved fiddly. Nevertheless, I made it with just a minute to spare and was greeted with cheers from the girls on duty. My last hour of frustration and stress must have shown on my red, sweaty face.

Inquiring about transportation to Byron, since I had no onward plans, the helpful staff suggested I use the car to drive to the airport drop off point nearby. They even checked bus times for me and gave me back the car key, allowing me to drop it off at this more convenient location.

After returning the car, I waited in the heat for twenty minutes for the next bus to arrive, by the time it came, I'd had enough time to contemplate whether it accepted card payments this time, recalling my previous experience. Once again, it turned out to be a cash-only bus fare of five dollars, which I fortunately had on hand, enabling me to enjoy a relaxing ride along the coast. I felt grateful I had chosen public transport, avoiding the stress that comes with a hire car.

The hotel I was heading to in Byron Bay was a bit different to my previous accommodations. I wanted my last few days alone in Australia to be perfect, so I splashed out a bit. The rooms were spacious, and mine came with a large balcony overlooking lush, well-established gardens. The hotel boasted a beautiful private pool and was just a stone's throw from the beach.

The hotel staff had emailed me that it was 'schoolies' time, an Australian term that refers to the end-of-year school holiday period when teenagers flock to the area. They assured me that their policy did not allow them to stay, which I appreciated, as their presence could have potentially disrupted my experience.

The last bus stop before Byron Bay reminded me

of the schoolies event as loads of over-excited girls in bikinis boarded with bags, food, rolled-up sleeping mats, and towels. In contrast, the floppy-haired boys wore shorts, no shirts or shoes, and carried just a phone tucked into their waistbands. As soon as I stepped off the bus, every road was bustling with young, exposed flesh and a fair share of older, weather-beaten individuals clad in loose, flowing, colourful clothes.

Byron Bay lived up to its reputation as a trendy hippie town, with an array of shops that catered to every imaginable taste. I couldn't help but think that most of these schoolies would return home with at least one tattoo and a crystal, and perhaps a broken heart. I found myself grateful that my own children were no longer teenagers!

The atmosphere was exciting and fresh, and I immediately felt content, eagerly anticipating the five days I had booked. Later that first afternoon, I made my way to the beach and relished the sight of more people than I had seen in a while. The crowd was diverse –

wide-eyed, awkward teenagers; hand-in-hand retirees; and young families enjoying picnics. Children with names like Silver and Summer were busy chasing seagulls. I was grateful to be somewhat invisible and blend into the background, as it allowed me to indulge in people-watching to my heart's content. As the bars began to come alive in the early evening, I decided to retreat to the safety of my balcony with a glass of wine and a pizza, listening to the unfolding chaos from afar.

Later that night, I was startled awake at midnight by a spectacular firework display over the bay, an unexpected treat on a warm Monday night. It was wonderful being in such a vibrant town, surrounded by life and energy, yet still having the option to have solitude and quiet whenever I wished.

I ventured down to the beach late morning on my first full day, where I again discovered the peace I had been longing for. The shoreline was almost deserted, as the youngsters obviously hadn't emerged for the day yet. I came to understand that grief evolves in stages, much like the pursuit of peace, each phase manifesting in different ways. Since Richard's passing, I had experienced different levels of acceptance. At two months, four months, and six months, I distinctly felt shifts in both my mental and physical well-being. By the eighth month, I found myself stabilising, less fixated on counting the days and weeks. This realisation made me feel a little melancholy, wondering if I still cared as much, and if I was losing some of the raw intensity of grief that I experienced earlier on.

Initially, I sought solitude, but now I find solace in observing people, particularly the younger generation. It's heartening to witness them embrace life with such enthusiasm, filled with dreams and aspirations. Their energy and optimism reminded me of Richard and our youthful days together. I cherished the time we had, grateful for the joy and laughter we had experienced along the way.

Of course, I saw it in a good light. I was well aware that the beauty of Byron was giving me such a positive outlook, but as this was the purpose of my entire trip, I wasn't going to apologise to myself for my aged hippie feeling of euphoria. Everyone had a reason to be there, and the beauty of this place made everything seem more manageable. People were celebrating, having fun, perhaps remembering, grieving, or just clearing their minds and seizing pure joy before making difficult life decisions. The truth was that every single person was getting on with their day, and that gave me my own personal comfort, seeing that time does go on, and mine will too.

I had been convinced that I needed to find inner peace before moving forward, and now it's becoming clear that this amazing country is working its magic on me. I would never have found this feeling so quickly if I had stayed home during the long, dark nights of the English winter. Little did I know, when we waved our daughter off to Australia 18 years ago, that her move would become my lifeline. It was the ideal place to escape to after my loss, a chance to run away under the guise of assisting her, though I'm sure she would have managed fine without me. I doubt I would have ventured so far without family connections.

I will never take this time of my life lightly or for granted. I'll forever be immensely grateful for the opportunity to do this, unrestricted and in such a stunning country. I've been blessed, and I won't shy away from acknowledging it as a privilege. This is my story, unique to me alone. Grief remains a constant, regardless of our actions, our location, or our coping mechanisms. True bravery, I believe, lies in the decisions we make after experiencing loss.

After my trip to the beach, I indulged in a solitary swim in the idyllic hotel pool. Quietly to myself, I made a pledge to seize every moment of my life, to care for our family, uphold Richard's memory, and treasure our shared experiences. I silently thanked him for making all of this possible. Nearby, a tiny gecko perched on the poolside rocks seemed to listen intently, tilting its head like a loyal Labrador, until it eventually lost interest in the lady with no food and scampered away. Nonetheless, it was comforting to have its company for a brief moment.

Afterwards, I returned to my room and cried. Tears flowed because I couldn't share the breathtaking beauty around me with the one person I longed for. They fell for the disbelief that I would never see him again or hear his voice. I cried out of loneliness, until my tears ran dry. That night, he appeared in my dreams, and I woke up angry at him for evoking memories of his fading voice and smile just when I thought I was moving forward. After harbouring frustration for a while, I smiled at the memory. With a lighter heart, I went back down to the beach in the dark and listened to the crashing waves until weariness finally allowed me to sleep.

Being in Australia feels like a temporary escape

from real life – a necessary reset for me. I can't expect to live every day like this, and gradually, I'm beginning to anticipate more typical pursuits – generating ideas, earning a living, and reconnecting with friends. This journey is a unique chapter in my life, fuelled by recent experiences and the emotions they've stirred within me. I recognise that it's been a rather drastic change, and naturally, there are days when I question my decision to be so far from home, knowing I must learn to navigate life alone.

I've even attempted to ease my grief by recalling the things I didn't like: the irritations, the bad habits, and the impractical ideas. I tried to knock him off his pedestal and paint him as the bad guy. I hoped this would help me stop missing him and allow me to revel in the relief of not having to deal with those things anymore. No more laundry for work clothes, no more struggling to come up with dinner ideas, no more constant sports on the television or mud tracked through the house. I tried to focus on all the positives of being alone, and it worked to some extent, until memories surfaced of his silly apologetic smile and blown kisses as he slowly reversed out of the lounge, leaving behind twice the amount of mud on the carpet.

September 2023…
Driftwood

…I'm not overwhelmed with unbearable grief anymore; the 'ending' brought me incredible pride, relief and overall peace. However, I am totally weakened by sadness. Tears fall freely, without drama, creating a wetness under my chin that I let drip until the tank has overflowed and the weight is bearable again. The effort of keeping a lid on my reservoir is far too great, and once the level gets too high, I take myself to a quiet place and turn on the tap.

Drifting through early grief is like a small branch bobbing steadily down a pretty, winding river. Sometimes it's a sunny day, warm and blue, cow parsley covering the bank, and the water is calm, moving towards an unknown destination. Silver light shimmers like jewels on the surface. Sunlight or moonlight it never ceases. Other times, the clouds are dark and menacing, spoiling the view. The river flows violently in all directions, and the solitary branch struggles to maintain stability, avoiding getting tangled in the reeds or bashing into the hidden rocks just below the choppy surface. Heading towards unknown waters, unable to get out of the course or pull over to the bank to catch a breath.

Will today bring fierce stormy weather and rapids, leaving me exhausted and battered, or will I gently float on top of a quiet millpond, alone in the warmth of the sun, appreciating the peace around me? Will I stay face up or roll face down?

Whatever each day brings is unknown until I open my eyes and remember I am that broken branch now, instead of being part of the tree I once was. That tall, blackened, lifeless silhouette still appears proud and strong after it dropped me into this river, and I now have to find my way through the rapids and ripples until I reach a more peaceful and familiar place. The dark, blue river courses through a colourless landscape like an unfinished painting by numbers. Maybe one day I'll be glad to get caught permanently in the riverbank, letting new life settle around and on me, giving me stability and a purpose once more.

All I really want to do is to fight my way back upstream with all my remaining strength and find my beautiful tree again, alive with leaves and birds, and reattach myself to it so we can be as one again. But I am no salmon, and the mighty oak is dead and bare now, getting further away from me each day. So, I'll try to accept myself as driftwood and see where the river of life takes me next.

Waking up with aggravated toothache again, likely from chewing on too many heavily toasted meals the day before, I took another painkiller and stayed in bed until the pain subsided. The convenience food available in places like this often consists of breaded items aimed at youngsters to soak up excess alcohol, which were also cheap and quick to buy. There were some lovely looking restaurants, but I still felt like a sad case being on my own, almost as if I had been stood up. So, it was easier to eat in cafés and pubs. However, because of my sore tooth, I did get funny looks when asking for room temperature drinks in such heat!

I had bought a piece of carrot cake on my first day, which was huge. I took the remnants back to the hotel, and since it was soft and appealing, it had already served as one supper and two breakfasts. While it was not nutritionally ideal, it was the right texture for my damaged tooth.

There was a terrific storm for most of the afternoon, and there is nothing more spectacular than a monsoon-style downpour. It brought out all the wildlife scuttling across the gardens. It was still hot enough to sit on the balcony in shorts and watch the rain smash through the greenery. Later, the sheet lightning almost soundlessly lit up the black sky over the sea.

The next day was cloudy with a fresher feel after the storm, so I decided to walk to the famous lighthouse, prepared this time with sunscreen and water. However, I wasn't ready for the steep paths in the growing heat once the sun broke through, meaning I lost concentration and found myself at sea level when I was supposed to be going up. The lighthouse was no nearer, and with my blister plasters beginning to curl, I chose to turn back, fearing I might get into difficulties as I had on my very first solo adventure.

I made the wise decision to trudge back to the hotel exhausted and went for a luxurious swim. For lunch, I picked up the nearest thing, another toastie. So, I never saw the lighthouse! However, I did see a lot more views of the bay, so my time wasn't completely wasted. I cooled down in my room, reading a book for the rest of the afternoon, before venturing to a nearby beachfront seafood restaurant that I had seen from my balcony.

There was a long, high table under the main open

window with lovely views over the sea a few metres away, making sitting alone much less obvious. The service was lovely, as was another seafood platter – my third this trip. Usually, I would avoid such dishes at home, afraid of more shell than flesh, but the Australian cuisine had so far been delicious, featuring a variety of fish in interesting formats without the padding of chips or bread. It was a very welcome change to my diet.

I wandered down to the shops late the next morning, still loving the vibe of the place. Without any need for a tattoo, bikini wax, flimsy top, or dreamcatcher, I headed instead to a small general store and decided to be sensible by buying a lunch of cheese, crackers, and olives, thinking it would be healthier and cheaper. Neither was true, as it happened, but it was a welcome change. However, I couldn't get the seafood platter from the previous night out of my head and decided I would eat there again later.

Keeping cool in my room, I checked out the TV and

ended up watching three hilarious episodes of vintage Baywatch before I stopped myself. Hotel TV choices can be a bit restrictive unless you have streaming accounts. I then wandered down to the sea again, taking it all in as if it were the first time I had seen it. I hoped I would never take it for granted, wanting the feeling I had craved many months before to become imprinted in my mind, so I could call on it anytime I felt sad.

I went into the seafood restaurant and was warmly greeted by the same waitress from the night before. She insisted she knew what I would order, having told her I'd be back for the same, and she got it exactly right, including the wine. Not bad for a very popular restaurant, even if it is expected of them. Her attention and kindness towards me were most welcome.

This time, I added a dessert, even though I'm not really a pudding person as they always come up huge (think carrot cake). But I had a feeling this was worth a try, and it was the nicest dessert I've had in a long time: a sensible amount of smooth vanilla ice cream with a hot espresso shot and a cream liqueur in another shot. Very satisfied, I went and sat on the grass looking out to sea for nearly an hour as it got dark. Again, lost in deep thought, I knew I would hold this place very dear in my heart. I realised I would be happy doing simple things again on my last day, instead of rushing around getting hot and flustered. The vast flocks of seagulls taking off in the moonlight were a thing to behold as the day closed.

My dream that night caused a setback as I had a vivid image of my husband waiting for me outside a bus station. Standing tall and handsome, alongside his brother for some reason, he smiled and waved to me. I was thrilled and started running to him, hesitating briefly as I felt a bit silly, knowing he was never one for over-the-top romantic gestures. Unable to stop myself, I ran harder, only to bloody wake up. In that one second before I woke, I had felt such relief, believing that life was normal again.

I tried desperately to lie still with my eyes closed, hoping to snatch him back, but it didn't work as my brain woke up and I felt the tears rolling over my nose. The dreams I was having were so vivid and always stirred me up. Throughout the day, I saw him, large as life, waving to me, but completely unreachable. I knew what he would have felt like and smelt like, and I could have guessed his words. I didn't like grief one little bit that morning. Maybe the dream was supposed to comfort me, but I could look at photos to see him whenever I chose. I didn't need to be thrown into fresh, moving images, making me believe he was getting on with his life, just without me.

November 2023...
Making good choices

...Accommodation while travelling is always interesting. My journey began with a very rough idea, only certain of the places where family schedules were involved. The rest of my itinerary felt almost like sticking a pin in a map. Though I knew I wanted to

follow the coast, I decided at least two stops should be a treat. So far, I hadn't made any considerable mistakes, but I had learnt how important location is and company websites with their reviews can't always be trusted.

Some places had me questioning where they took their promotional photos – showing large pools, nearby beaches, and lovely rooms. They had definitely used a certain amount of artistic licence. However, I've never been disappointed by the size and cleanliness of the rooms, the toiletries supplied, or the staff. All the beds have been perfect, and though Australian television takes some getting used to and the reception isn't always great, I've made the best of it. The downloaded content on my iPad, as suggested by my daughter, has been invaluable.

The optimum time to stay in a decent hotel is four or five nights. A basic hotel is tolerable for two nights, and staying with friends should also be about two, maybe three nights. Couch surfing depends entirely on how well you know your hosts. Two days is usually enough for welcome conversation, shared meals, and a recce around the area. It's always better to leave wanting more than to overstay your welcome.

Even quiet places of solitude have their limits, as the novelty wears off once you've looked in every drawer and cupboard and checked out the food and wine available. This raises the question: Do you buy provisions before you get there, hope there's a shop nearby, go without, or risk waste by having things go off in your hot backpack? These are all things to consider when planning a trip.

I could have spent longer in Bicheno, but that was based more on emotions than practicality. There was nothing to do, which was perfect because, at that time, I fiercely wanted to be alone. My writing had taken off and was proving almost addictive, so although another day would have been welcome, I would have needed more to eat, which would have broken the spell.

I stayed too long in the first hotel room in Hobart, but that was no one's fault but my own; I didn't ask the questions I would now, such as, 'What is the view?' and 'Do the windows open?' Embracing the element of risk in choosing accommodations is quite enjoyable, especially in exploring a new hotel room and making it feel like home after unpacking. It's also easy to tidy up and repack in just a few minutes before leaving. A balcony is always a bonus, it can absolutely enhance the experience if you want to spend peaceful time in your room.

The chalet in Port Macquarie would not have been as enjoyable without the small general store and beach in close proximity. It was probably the most misleading accommodation in terms of location, but I lucked out with that one, avoiding any dreadful mistakes.

My decision to hire a car for only two sections of my trip proved correct, mainly due to the efficient public transport system, which allowed me to save enough money to spend on my 'luxury' accommodation. This trip isn't strictly a holiday in the usual sense, so I'm bound to have a different take. Still, I know I will look back on these few weeks as precious and vital to my healing.

My toothache had finally subsided, and, for whatever reason, had got better on its own. It made no sense at all, as it had reached the point where I considered ripping it out myself. How I returned to being pain-free and able to eat and drink normally again baffled me, but I was delighted and hoped it remained this way, at least until I got home.

I was picked up by a friend from Byron at midday, just as I was observing the same youngsters I had arrived with, dragging their feet and dreamcatchers back to the bus and, presumably, back to their parents' houses to mend their broken hearts. We drove an hour north to Elanora, on the Gold Coast. It was hot and humid, but a beautiful day. My host very kindly showed me around the local area before we went for drinks and dinner. It was nice to have company again, and I felt my need for solitude fading. However, knowing I could enjoy my own company made me feel more prepared for the journey home in a few weeks.

Over the next few days, I was shown the highlights of the Gold Coast area, from Tamborine Mountain to the beaches of Surfers Paradise. It's a beautiful area to visit, and I enjoyed true home comforts generously shared by my friend. Three days later, with fresh clothes packed, I took a train to a Brisbane Airport hotel. I had an early flight booked the following morning to Auckland, on the North Island of New Zealand. My room had a massive window overlooking the runway, so I spent the evening happily watching planes take off and land, enjoying a beautiful sunset with wine and a sandwich.

I had a good night's sleep, interrupted by my alarm at 5 a.m. to get the shuttle bus for the five-minute ride to the airport, where I endured two hours of preflight procedures. A full security check, being an international flight to New Zealand, meant almost all my luggage was pulled apart as they were convinced I had drill bits in my bag, according to the scanner, which turned out to be a pair of tweezers. Adding to the excitement, my arm's fat layer turned up on the drug X-ray, giving me a complex about my apparent body deformity on my left-hand side. Note to self: wear supportive underwear before an international flight!

April 2022...

Keeping it real

...Dark humour has been vital in helping us cope. Comments about looking for a new, rich husband, wondering whether to bother ironing his shirts, suggesting funny and inappropriate funeral songs have become our way of lightening the mood.

Nothing nasty just a light-hearted take on our world. These stories, when shared with friends, often resulted in a mix of of shock and relief, but they always manage to lift our spirits, even if just between the two of us. Finding a way to smile and laugh is far better than revealing true emotions, which only leads to tears or bitten lips. So why not have a giggle about it all and break the ice? Shedding tears while laughing is a strange but comforting feeling and much easier than holding them back.

There are always the comments that hit harder: 'Well, there's another grandchild I'll never meet', 'Better not book flights yet', or 'I'll do that job in the garden next year... if I'm still alive'. These thoughts constantly cross our minds, but we have learnt to say them out loud rather than letting them fester. It's a skill that I believe is better shared and definitely helps to dilute the hard facts.

Attending funerals and seeing the process unfold, knowing it could be me and the children in the dreaded front pew, is difficult. However, these awkward experiences open the door to honest conversations. Talking about other people's similar issues is easier than discussing our own.

These snippets of conversation gradually reveal true feelings and small details that help clarify the future and show us the direction we are heading. I understand there is no point trying to draw feelings out of a reluctant person until there is something concrete and important to discuss. But it's surprising how light-hearted comments can give you a window into someone else's mind.

I make a point of remembering or jotting down the bits of information I glean, such as definite likes and dislikes for a funeral and what he wants us to do. There's a lot I don't need to bother him with, and the fact he trusts me to do the right thing is approval enough. I know I can ask crucial things if I pick the right time. Once answered, they are put away comfortably in his head again, while I discreetly note them down.

The flight into New Zealand was magical. The coastline, the sky, and the clouds created a scene I will always remember. With music I loved playing in my ears, I felt fortunate once again to be on this journey. After a slight delay in Auckland, followed by a surprisingly smooth propeller flight to New Plymouth, I was greeted emotionally by my youngest son Nicholas, his wife, and their one year old daughter. They were visiting her Kiwi family for Christmas from England, as a last minute arrangement and it proved to be great addition to my trip to 'pop' over to New Zealand to see them all and meet her family.

From the air, I could see it was a beautiful country, with its mountainous regions and coastline being very reminiscent of Tasmania. Bringing the Australian sunshine with me, I spent a lovely five days with them. Seeing family again was a highlight and a relief. I could truly be myself with the people I loved most; I didn't have to pretend or exchange pleasantries. I could just talk freely and openly, sharing my grief to some extent with people who fully understood. After a long evening of heartfelt conversation, and revelling in each other's company, we all settled down. The next day, I took a backseat as they showed me around their part of the world. I couldn't have been happier!

It was a refreshing change to be the guest instead of the planner. They took me to various accommodations they had chosen and showed me places they wanted me to see, allowing me to fully relax for a few days. The lifestyle appeared as laid-back as Australia, but in a greener and slightly cooler setting. The roads were easy to navigate, the people were kind, the food delicious, and the countryside amazing. I would have loved more time to explore the east coast and South Island, but I had a feeling I would return some day.

We embarked on a five-day journey from New Plymouth, with the magnificent Mount Taranaki in the background, down to Wellington at the very bottom of North Island. Leaving the main road and venturing precariously over the mountain range was exciting but scary, especially because a fallen tree blocked the road right at the end, forcing us to backtrack and navigate the route once more!

We spent two days in Wellington and climbed Mount Victoria, which offered panoramic views of the bays, airport, and historic buildings. Despite being a relatively quiet capital city, it evoked a real sense of history.

We visited the Te Papa Museum, which had a fantastic display about New Zealand's role in the Gallipoli campaign, incredibly well put together and leaving me in tears for all those who went through such hardship and sacrifice. The museum also provided informative exhibitions on the local wildlife and the eye-opening reality of the earthquakes in New Zealand. It highlighted the geological risk of living on a fault line, which spans both islands. Seeing 'Earthquake Prone Area' notices in restaurant windows underneath the menus was a little off-putting!

My eighth flight of 14, from Wellington back to Brisbane, was just as thrilling as the others. However, the wait in the airport nearly matched the flight's duration, as a full storm blew through, complete with thunder and lightening, delaying the flight by two hours. Wellington is renowned for fast-changing and often windy weather, and it was incredible how quickly it went from calm sunshine to an absolute torrent, only to clear up again soon after. The silver lining was that I had a complete row of seats to myself on the plane, though others weren't so fortunate and had their flights cancelled entirely.

I've learnt to plan for these inevitable waits, and most airports offer good views of the runway, a bar or café, something to eat and read, and plenty of people-watching opportunities. I also began carrying my iPad in my handbag so I could write during the downtime. Consequently, the time passed quite easily in airport lounges, and so far, I've only encountered

brief delays. I wondered if I would be lucky enough to complete the remainder of my fourteen flights without incident.

I was sad to leave my son and family to become a solo traveller again, but those few days with them had done me so much good. I was glad our trips overlapped briefly, and I took comfort in knowing I would see them at home in a few weeks. Back at the Brisbane Airport hotel, I spent another evening watching the busy runway at sunset, as I had done the week before.

My solo six-week trip had worked very well, and I felt more confident about my future as I prepared to finally return home in the new year. I had experienced moments of great joy and deep, heavy sadness, but it had to be done, and there's no doubt in my mind that I did the right thing, in the right place. I was aware it would still be hard to walk back into my house alone, in the dark and cold of an English winter, but I'll never forget my weeks of peace and solitude in the sun. The weather was such a major plus, and spending time with two of my children was a massive bonus.

The morning before I had to leave my Brisbane hotel room, I had the opportunity to reflect on my trip, watching the early morning flights take off. So far, I had seen eight cities from the air, each unique in its own way, but sharing the common feature of a nearby coastline. Observing miles and miles of beautiful stretches of sand with the sea crashing against the shore, often unseen by anyone except aeroplane passengers, put the whole of Australia and New Zealand into perspective.

As I write this, Led Zeppelin's *'Ramble On'* is on my playlist, its well-timed words making me smile. The plans for this past six-week solo trip had occupied the forefront of my mind for so long, keeping the thoughts of real life at bay. Now, with home drawing nearer, I feel a bit apprehensive. I don't want to feel sad again, but it's inevitable. I have no option other than to follow the great lyrics and keep moving forward. The gist, as the title suggests, is to be grateful for the time I've had travelling, but now I have to face up to the journey home and impending pain. I need to keep going forward with confidence and courage.

Ramble: *'when you keep walking on and on and on, in no hurry to make a point or get to a destination – if there is one at all'.*

How beautiful and apt. This little unexpected nugget gave me a real spring in my step. I hopped on to the plane with the warmth of achievement in my bones, as I flew back to Perth to spend the last three weeks of my trip, including the Christmas period, with my daughter and her family.

Had I caught the bug for travel? Maybe to some extent, but what I truly gained was newfound confidence in being by myself. I've never been afraid to book things, fly, or stay in various accommodations, I've always found those things exciting. The real challenge was being alone. Now, I would like to travel more, not only for an annual visit to see my daughter but to explore more of Western Australia instead of just the east coast. I'll also consider other destinations, but since comfortable accommodation is not cheap, I will have to earn some money before I get too excited about new adventures.

Exploring more of the British Isles is very appealing, especially the South West Coast Path, which inspired me initially and again in Tasmania. The Highlands of Scotland have always been appealing, and the coasts of the Isle of Wight and the Channel Islands may well draw me in. I've visited both before, but I would love to see different island coastlines. Wherever I head, I feel the coast will often be my chosen path.

I've still got to go through the process of being at home alone first, and I can't keep running away. I need to manage day-to-day life, so it's one step at a time. This journey has been a significant part of my healing, and while it's shown me the joy of exploring new places, it's also taught me the importance of finding peace within myself, no matter where I am.

December 2022…
Mum

…I haven't mentioned my mother much, apart from
noting that she passed away just three months before
my husband. She was very old and died as peacefully
as one can at that age, in the nursing home where I
worked. She had moved there five years earlier, and it
was my privilege to reconnect with her and spend time
together. I was able to see her every day, even during the
pandemic, and for that, I'm eternally grateful. She was
a truly wonderful mother, and I miss her dearly, though
it's a different kind of grief.

I had stopped living with her many years ago, moving
straight into the arms of my husband, so I never felt the
loneliness I do now. Of course, the two relationships
were completely different, and the grief I feel for her
is distinct, but blurred into one overwhelming sense of
loss. Knowing their health issues, I had always feared
that there wouldn't be much time between their deaths.
It was especially hard not being able to confide in my

mother as my husband deteriorated because I knew it would break her heart to see me struggling, as she was unable to care for me like she had when I was a child.

Despite being bedridden, she still had the ability to read me like a book. She couldn't do much to help me or even hug me like any other mother. I had to pretend everything was normal, which was not easy since Richard worked at the same nursing home. I could tell by her eyes that she was slowly figuring it out. I was relieved she passed peacefully before him, giving me just enough time to give her the love and respect she deserved.

With both of them gone, I took early retirement, a huge relief. Working in a place with so many memories was incredibly hard, and seeing the kind-hearted staff who had lost a long term colleague and a popular resident was equally challenging.

Chapter 3

Turbulence

Returning to Perth and family was a soothing balm after my whirlwind journey. It was comforting to unpack and settle into familiar surroundings, with fresh clothes, a stocked fridge, and a full bowl of fruit on the table – simple things I had missed, despite the relatively short time away. Being back with family made me feel vulnerable yet again, although comforted.

For a few days, I didn't feel well. The toll of a poor diet, dehydration, jet lag, and emotional exhaustion had caught up with me. After all, I had changed my watch six times in six weeks. Once I started eating properly and drinking more water, I began to feel better. One of my persistent problems is worrying about the availability of toilets while travelling, which often leads to a low intake of liquids.

With that concern alleviated, I began to look forward to celebrating a 30+°C Christmas and New Year in the coming weeks. The chance to unwind and prepare for the last leg leading up to the festive season was refreshing. The stark contrast to England's Christmas was striking, but not just because of the scorching heat. The Australian attitude was remarkably calmer, devoid of the last-minute frantic rush I was accustomed to.

In Australia, the main day revolved around mostly cold food enjoyed in an outdoor setting, often with the strong possibility of a swim in the pool once the meal had settled. This was a far cry from the traditions I grew up with. With cosy indoor settings, hot meals, and the hustle and bustle of preparations. Yet, this first hot Christmas was a welcome change for me personally, and I found myself becoming converted to the idea of celebrating in a warmer climate. The relaxed atmosphere allowed me to embrace the season differently, finding joy in new traditions while appreciating being surrounded by family. This blend of new and old made for a uniquely special holiday season, marking another step in my journey of healing and adaptation.

My emotions were heightened after a series of events that had unfolded in the New Year. I had a heartfelt conversation with Catherine about her last visit to see her dad in the hospice. This stirred up my own feelings as he had requested that I wasn't there when he passed. So, after a very emotional goodbye, two days before he died, I never saw him again. However, our son and daughter chose to visit him, with my blessing. She gently explained that he would have hated me being there and vice versa, as he hadn't been keen on even doctors seeing him, let alone family. He had received the children's last visit awkwardly, his stoicism in facing his death so typical of him. After that chat, I felt very relieved.

On a much brighter note, I was invited to visit the high-rise offices of Subsea 7 in the centre of Perth's business district in respect of some work Richard had instigated a year before his death. I was kindly shown around the offices and took photos of the fantastic view over the Swan River and Elizabeth Quay, guided by a young Englishman, who shared my opinion of what constituted a real rush hour – not the brief queue of ten cars we could see on the bridge far below, which the Australians considered an inconvenience! My husband had been very passionate about the work collaboration, and I was keen to do this visit in his memory. It was a nice change to my day, relighting my interest in real life. I had something important to do and felt like a contributing adult again.

April 2023…
Sign of the times…

…I have always been very open-minded about signs from the dead, a belief that was solidified after

the first major loss of my dad nearly twenty years ago. The day after my dear father passed away, I drew two big kisses, a double XX, on my shower's steamy window while crying hard in the spray. Later that bright, frosty day, while walking my dog, I saw a huge XX, carved across the blue sky by high-flying aeroplanes. It was an uncommon pattern in a sky with many plane trails, but clear as anything. From that day, whenever I see plane trails cross, I smile, knowing my dad is looking over me. I also remember hearing the song Strangers in the Night played over the radio at the exact moment, I later found out, that he passed away – one of his most favourite songs.

I take signs more seriously now, not dismissing them as fantasies, coincidences, tricks of the mind, or simply grasping at straws. I am not an airy-fairy person, but when my husband died, his presence was incredible, and it gave me great comfort. Nobody was going to take that away from me with their negative or doubtful responses.

Of course, the music we shared would play on my playlist at pertinent moments, but it was bound to come around sooner or later. In those first awful weeks of grief, all I wanted was comfort, and I was determined to grab every piece of it. Candles blew out at poignant times, feathers appeared when tears fell, and doves landed in the garden. Each time, I felt lifted and honoured. It wasn't just me; colleagues at work told me of incontestable incidents, making all of us shiver and smile. These signs faded over time, but I took great comfort from them and enjoyed something positive for a change.

A couple of days before Richard died, I was given a small amethyst from a thoughtful friend. I have always loved this crystal as it is my favourite colour, purple, and also my birthstone. I know they have possible healing properties, but my main reason for liking them was their shape and colour as a pretty trinket.

During our last hours together, I decided to hold

this crystal between both our hands, hoping to imbue it with our energy, spirit, or whatever essence I could grasp. I was desperate to keep something tangible of him, so he indulged me until I gripped his hand too tightly, and he remarked that the crystal was a bit sharp. I kept it safe and later made it into a necklace that I wear every day, so I have some small token to carry with me.

After my visit to the Perth office, I took the bus home. I went to my usual seat, as it offered the best views of the city, and found a small, white feather on it. I didn't care about its origins but to me, it was a sign that he was pleased I had made that visit for him. I felt proud, happy, and delighted, especially since I had accepted that all signs had probably dried up, given that he was a man of few grand gestures. I smiled and put the feather in my pocket.

The following day, I decided to place some of his ashes, which I wanted to travel with and give to my daughter, at a beautiful waterfall spot, Lesmurdie

Falls, overlooking the Perth skyline and surrounding area. This represented our Australian connection and gave my daughter and family a solid place to visit in the future. I had wanted to do this, as all his other ashes were scattered in important areas. I chose a pile of fixed boulders, with one just loose enough that I could move it a bit to make a gap. I placed the ashes there, right in front of a small quandong tree with a blackened trunk, offering a perfect view for miles.

Initially, I did not like the idea of splitting his ashes up, but since his wish was to go up in a firework, he had already changed my thinking. I knew he would be chuffed with the idea, rather than being confined to a box. To date, his ashes have been sent off from a mountain in the Lake District, gone up in six fireworks near our house, and now, he overlooks the Perth skyline and airport. Every time I take off and land, I can look over to the slabs of rocks, quandong trees, and boulders, knowing he will look after our daughter and be there whenever one of us visits. The bulk of the ashes are still at home, as I'm not ready to let them all go yet, if at all.

December 2023…
The blackened tree

…That night, I had the strongest, most vivid, and pertinent dream of him since he died. I could touch him, hold him, laugh with him, cajole him, and finally tell him just how much I loved him. He wore shirts he had owned years ago, his hair was thick and beautiful, his shoulders strong and broad, his smile real, and his comments typical and silly as ever. He was tall and handsome, just as I remembered him before his illness. At the end of this perfect dream, he stood in front of a blackened tree, looking seriously into the distance, an identical setting of where I had placed his ashes the day before, with the gentle sound of bagpipes playing in the background. As I hugged him hard and said how much I would miss him, he dropped his head with sad eyes and disappeared. I woke up crying, feeling shocked, happy, sad, and completely taken aback, and I sobbed for an hour as I came to terms with these mixed feelings.

I hadn't listened to the bagpipe music he had requested to play at the end of his funeral for ages, yet there it was, the soundtrack of this dream. I took Rescue Remedy to help calm the strength of my emotions, ones I hadn't felt so strongly since the day he died. I wanted a photo of that moment; I wished I could sketch the scene. I couldn't bear to forget it as it was so vivid in detail.

The moment reinforced my belief that he was still around, and eventually, I felt only happiness and a new strength. That's really all I could hope for from this journey of mine, and I believe, in that moment, I had found peace with my loss and drawn a somewhat wobbly line under it.

A few days later, we drove down to Margaret River, 170 miles south of Perth, for the new year and a change of scene. It's a lovely small town, reminiscent of Byron Bay but aimed more at families rather than backpackers, with interesting shops for tourists and only a short drive to the beach. The landscape is dominated by numerous, often vast, wineries, many with a historic story of businesses passed down through generations. This proves that the lovely weather and terrain are perfect for the well-known wine industry in the area. It's a beautiful region that I would love to spend more time exploring another time.

So, I welcomed the new year quietly, struck with the thought of this being the first one I had to navigate alone. Since returning to Perth, my ideas of what to do next had been growing, thankfully, and although the year ahead seemed daunting, my positivity held strong. I knew I had to continue what I was doing – surviving. Thinking it, feeling it, embracing it, and acting upon it – 'it' being life. With the time I have left, I aim to do my best, always remembering to be grateful for this chance.

I would be home in two weeks, and this escape, however I dressed it up, would come to an end. The earlier fear of returning to England had diminished over these past four months. I was beginning to have practical ideas of decorating the house, moving furniture, decluttering, and essentially making it my own. I didn't feel guilty about this now. No doubt I would feel sadness when it came to do it, but as I had no desire to move house, making it my own seemed like a positive step forward.

In a few days, I would be in Mauritius, an island off the East African coast for a two-day extended stopover en route to Durban, South Africa. There, I would be staying with my sister for a week before flying back home from Johannesburg, South Africa. It wasn't a straightforward connection, but I was excited to see another country. After a three-week break, I was happy to fly again. The weather looked promising in both places, and I felt lucky to have escaped the severe weather on the east coast of Australia that struck shortly after I left for Perth. It was heartbreaking to see places I had witnessed in beautiful conditions, only weeks earlier, being ripped apart under destructive conditions of wind and rain. Similar weather was also affecting the UK, more expected perhaps at this time

of year, but difficult to watch from afar.

Mauritius greeted me with intense heat, like stepping into an oven, despite the pouring rain, thunder, and lightning. Thankfully, the plane had landed just minutes before the deluge began. However, the subsequent taxi ride to the villa turned into an hour-long, white-knuckle journey I could have done without. When I did catch glimpses of the view at dusk, it was of an amazing flashing orange and grey sky, revealing impressive mountains and a beautiful sunset.

With my broken, schoolgirl French failing to provide any means of communication with the driver, I couldn't plead for either air conditioning or windscreen demisting to clear our vision towards potential disaster. Perhaps the rivers of sweat running into my eyes were a small blessing. Eventually, the monsoon cleared, the demisters were located, and after much pulling over to loudly ask locals for directions, being aggressively honked at as he stopped in the middle of main roads, and several dangerous U-turns later, I arrived at the villa in the darkness. Thankfully, the owner had kindly come to find and guide us in.

My room was lovely, spacious, and clean with a large balcony overlooking a pretty, serene pool and swaying palm trees. Having booked this in the early days of my plans, before I had become more of a seasoned traveller, I soon realised I had made two obvious mistakes. Firstly, I needed to eat, and secondly, this was a stopover, not a holiday. I should have booked accommodation closer to the airport instead of wasting time and adding unnecessary stress by driving an hour away. Consulting a map, I spotted several nice beach accommodations just a few kilometres from the airport. Lessons learnt for next time.

Although I had foreseen that no food would be provided, my focus on the heart-stopping drive meant that I had overlooked this, leading me to skip dinner. The following morning, I braved the local supermarket

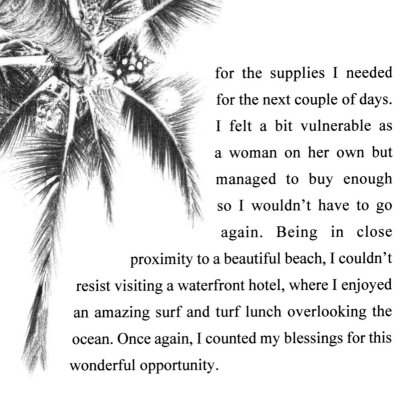

for the supplies I needed for the next couple of days. I felt a bit vulnerable as a woman on her own but managed to buy enough so I wouldn't have to go again. Being in close proximity to a beautiful beach, I couldn't resist visiting a waterfront hotel, where I enjoyed an amazing surf and turf lunch overlooking the ocean. Once again, I counted my blessings for this wonderful opportunity.

I did experience a momentary sadness, the familiar feeling of not sharing the experience with anyone stung. Yet, booking a table for one and dining alone was becoming less strange. The food was fantastic, and the location resembled a film set with its bright blue sea lapping about 20 feet from my table. I felt the spirit and allure of the island, enjoying the peace and quiet for the chance to write.

Reflecting on future trips back from Australia, Mauritius will likely become a regular stop-off, so I will book a hotel nearer the airport and on the beach if possible, purely to avoid so much travel. On the upside, I cleared the airport X-ray without any body shaming!

The return journey to the airport was much more pleasant, allowing me to appreciate the island's scenery, particularly its majestic mountains. Mauritius is a very pretty island, and I look forward to visiting again one day.

However, I was beginning to grow weary of airports. While I don't mind the flying itself and have been fortunate that most of my flights have gone ahead without major incident, the process is laborious. Every airport operates much the same way, and after spending countless hours killing time in duty-free shops and café, the novelty has worn off. Nonetheless, I think the airport staff do a terrific job keeping the numerous planes on time and the stressed passengers comfortable, for the most part. Famous last words.

Unfortunately, shortly after I left, bad weather caught up with this beautiful island. I saw distressing images on the news of the airport packed with stranded passengers as hurricanes battered Mauritius. Having experienced some inclement weather there, I could only begin to imagine how terrifying and destructive the storms must have been.

The flight to Johannesburg was delayed by an hour, which ate into the time I had before my connection to Durban. As a result, I arrived much later than planned. Interestingly, the original connecting flight had to return to Johannesburg due to technical issues, so I avoided that hassle at least. With no means of communication, my sister spent many hours unsure of when or if I would arrive, but eventually, I did. After a nerve-wracking three-hour drive in the dark, we reached my nephew's house. I began to question whether I would choose this route again in the future.

The following day, I was treated to a fantastic and relaxing African lodge and spa experience in a beautiful bush setting for the night. It was quite a novelty being watched by a couple of curious grey monkeys during my outdoor shower, but the food was delicious, and it was a joy to revisit South Africa after 20 years.

The next day brought a completely different camping experience as we joined my nephews and their families for their annual new year holiday at Cape Vidal on the east coast, just over an hour from their house. They had set up a homemade camp in a game reserve, featuring several interconnected tents, a camp kitchen, and a large central dining area covered by a large canvas canopy.

The setting offered a true camping experience amidst nature, with sightings of game such as buffalo, nyala, leopard, kudu, and impala. Alongside these magnificent creatures were smaller ones, such as hyenas, monkeys, honey badgers, cockroaches, spiders, huge ants, mosquitoes, and the occasional tick.

Cape Vidal, a World Heritage site, had breathtaking views of the crashing Indian Ocean, impressive giant sand dunes, expansive white beaches, and the vast blue sky. As evenings rolled into nights, the space was filled with the noise of birds, frogs, and various insects attempting to claim their territory, creating a thoroughly immersive experience. The grand finale was a massive thunder and lightning storm on our last night, adding to the dramatic atmosphere of South Africa in all its glory.

The next day involved reorganisation and packing up as the families prepared to return to their daily routines, while travellers like myself had to brush off the sand, tend to the latest mosquito bite, pack the trusty backpack, and continue the journey home. I knew I would miss the vastness and clarity of nature that these countries, which I had been fortunate to visit, offered the light, the space, the laid-back attitude towards life, and the friendliness of strangers. The warmth was an obvious draw, although I found the humidity oppressive. Back home, the forecast predicted grim, cold weather, with recent snow potentially affecting my flight. However, I pushed aside those thoughts for the moment and focused on the view before me, absorbing every minute.

I had relished crossing nations, experiencing different lifestyles and cultures, witnessing changing weather patterns, and observing how my immediate and extended family spent their days, nurturing their hopes and dreams. It all felt beautifully connected, and I couldn't help but smile with satisfaction and gratitude for my journey. This experience was born out of extenuating circumstances and the opportunities seized during a difficult time.

Overall, it was a chance to heal and move forward positively, striving to do my best in the years ahead. I couldn't escape the feeling that if the beauty and vastness of our natural world didn't contribute to healing a damaged soul, then perhaps nothing could.

The final journey was both hot and exhausting, involving a long drive to the airport followed by a one-hour connection, navigating through all the necessary hurdles. I desperately wanted to be on board the final, fourteenth flight bound for England.

Remarkably, I seemed to have stayed one step ahead of horrendous weather conditions along the way, which persisted until I touched down at Heathrow. I had departed Perth only to hear about a massive heatwave hitting the city a few days later. Similarly, after leaving the Gold Coast, it was struck by severe storms, flooding, and destruction. I departed New Zealand just after terrible weather struck. Even after enjoying beautiful weather in Mauritius, the island was ravaged by a devastating hurricane that cut off the airport and caused severe damage. As the plane ascended from Johannesburg, I looked out of the window and watched sheet lightning slice through the gathering, dark clouds, momentarily illuminating the sprawling city below.

Watching news reports from around the world took on a deeper meaning for me as I saw familiar places devastated by natural disasters. While I felt fortunate to have personally missed these calamities, it gave me a profound perspective on global weather patterns and their impact on beautiful places and the local communities.

Adding up the distances, I had covered approximately 30,000 miles, which is 5,000 more than the length of the equator. The six different airline companies had provided me with professional and comfortable transport. I had enjoyed incredible local food served by considerate people who never questioned my single status. I met kind-hearted people everywhere I went and witnessed views and forces of nature that I will never, ever forget.

This experience has nourished my soul and begun to heal my heart. Thank you to every single person involved for making it so special.

Chapter 4

The Landing

For some reason, I was upgraded to Premium Economy on my final flight, and I appreciated the extra legroom and small comfort it provided. Throughout the entire trip, however, there was a lingering thought in the back of my mind: what would it be like to step back into my life after such an adventure, or rather, my escape from reality? Truthfully, I was delighted to be seeing my family again, breathing the chilled air, and being surrounded by familiar roads and countryside.

After being collected by my son from Heathrow Airport, pulling into the lane I had a warm feeling of joy and relief seeing my house and car again. Now I could relax with my home comforts around me. Yet, I did feel slightly unwell with chills, aches, and pains for a day or two, which I again attributed to the effects of air travel, emotions, and perhaps relief. However, after a few good nights' sleep in my own bed, I felt fine.

The reality truly began to sink in after those initial days when I re-read condolence cards, sniffed clothes in the wardrobes, and shed heavy tears. Despite the emotional weight, it still felt much easier being alone after having dealt with it for the past five months. I saw the house as mine for the first time, and it all just felt okay. Not great, but a positive kind of okay – an improvement from how it felt before I had left. I even lowered the bathroom mirror, by several inches, originally installed to accommodate my 6'4" husband 30 years ago. I could now see the whole of my face instead of just the top of my head!

January 2024...
No hiding now

...You don't have a shadow anymore; the sun

shines solely on me now. Yours was a strong, large shadow that I loved sharing, protecting me from the glare of life and shielding me from the real person I was underneath. Now, fully exposed to life's harsh light, I can no longer hide in your shadow.

I never minded being there; I was always true to myself, happy, and honoured to share your space. But now, as I navigate life alone, I am slowly getting used to this new reality and feeling less overwhelmed. I am learning more about myself, proud of what I've accomplished since your death, and seeing life from a different perspective. Without the constant, rubber band cycle of your cancer treatments, every step I take is a step forward. I revisit our sweet memories through photos and letters, considering this a necessary part of my journey forward, not a step back.

The vast emptiness that appeared after you were gone is gradually filling with new experiences and opportunities. My future is taking shape, marked by the freedom of choices and decisions once postponed and put on the back burner to manage family life. Now, these pursuits carry a hint of excitement rather than mere survival.

I deeply miss discussing and debating life's issues; deciding everything without your input feels strange. Imagining what you would say offers comfort, but it's not the same.

I am learning, and as much as I wish I could be sheltered by your shadow once more, I will face the sun and do my best to shine. Thank you, my tall, handsome man for always looking after me.

Chapter 5

Baggage Claim

When all the plans for the trip were coming together, I never really considered how I would feel afterwards. At the time, my mind was too full to contemplate it, and I believed there was no point in guessing how I might feel. I would just cross that bridge when the time came. Well, that time has now come. I've been back just over five weeks, and the initial excitement has eased. The first emotional trough has passed, the bedroom is now mine, and friends and family have grown accustomed to my return. Now, I'm in it for the long haul. Home had changed irrevocably.

Slowly, I began to reorganise our bedroom. It was the bed where he had often rested, the covers I had changed after sweaty or sickly nights, and the ceiling we had both stared at in silence, deep in our own thoughts about the future. (I had slept in the spare room during his illness to avoid disturbing him) I had the walls painted and different carpet fitted. I was gradually moving back in, step by step – an adjustment I couldn't have imagined making earlier, but now it felt fine to do so. Each time I moved something of his, I silently apologised to him, expressing regret for having to make these changes, though most of his belongings were only going across the landing into the spare room. Finally, I pushed our bed right under the window, which offered a beautiful and familiar view over the fields that gave comfort of the 30 years we had shared. Removing his bedside table, as so obviously bare and unused. I now slept on his side of the bed for closeness.

Once, I found myself wiping the paintwork on a door, a simple job but stopped abruptly, realising I might be erasing his touch. It was something I had never considered before, so for now, the door frames will remain as they are. They don't mention this in support manuals. His toiletries were all gone except for the last can of deodorant, which I sprayed every morning to remind me of the only scent I had left of him. I wouldn't replace it once empty, wary that it could become an unbreakable habit.

August 2023...
The lost cufflinks

...Something in me decided to clear out the bulk of your clothes quite early on. The ones I disliked or that held no sentimental value were easy to part with. A charity van collected six huge bin liners, ensuring that someone in another country could wear the Christmas suits and the numerous T-shirts you collected from everywhere you visited. I didn't want them to stay locally in case I saw them on the high street one day.

I kept a bag of my favourite items and plan to have keepsake teddy bears made for the grandchildren, and perhaps a cushion for myself. Your inimitable style will live on, I promise.

Some drawers were easy to clear, filled with rubbish and broken things you couldn't throw away. But other drawers were awful to go through, filled with personal items only you had chosen to put there. No secrets, just your stuff. We all have stuff, and I hated the thought of people rifling through mine. It felt wrong and deceitful, as if I were exposing a hidden past. I found all the used contact lenses you lazily dropped into your bedside drawer, but it wasn't hard getting rid of the bottles of various skin creams you bought in the hope they might relieve the horrible effects of chemo.

The easiest task was clearing out most of the numerous mugs you refused to give up, the dried-up shoe polish you insisted on keeping, and so many other 'just in case' items. The endless mismatched plates kept from your parent's house, along with a loft full of other useless and worthless items, also went. That felt good. I didn't want the children to have that burden later on, having cleared two houses of our parents' accumulated stuff over the years. I wanted to choose how our things were disposed of. Getting rid of material items was relatively easy, but handling and smelling your clothes for the last time was gutwrenching, and I cried a lot, feeling as if I were erasing you from my life completely. Even the things I chose to keep were moved into a spare room, the last evidence that we ever shared the main bedroom.

I'll never get rid of my favourite shirt, and I'll wear your T-shirts to bed to feel close to you. Your precious hats will always hang on the pegs in the hall. Searching through pockets and drawers, I found all your lost cufflinks and put them in a bowl on the bedroom windowsill, just in case. At least now you know where they are if you ever need them.

The early retirement I never expected years ago now brought a mixed feeling of both happiness and sadness, difficult to face, almost easier to avoid. All my old colleagues would be going to work, following the routine that had dictated our lives for so long. But now I could stay in bed until midday if I wanted to, nobody was expecting me anywhere, and I had nowhere to be. It was a strange mix of peace, pointlessness, and sadness, knowing that even if well-earned, this retirement also wouldn't have been possible if Richard had lived. It was yet another new feeling I had to get used to, as the euphoria of returning home wore off, the harsh reality of my life remained.

The weekends were the hardest days, not for a lack of invitations out, but because they were the days when he would normally be around more. Coffee and breakfast together, arrangements made for a night out, jobs done in the garden, or more likely, him just watching yet more cricket on the television while I cooked. The companionable chat, humour, and gentle silences as we both went about our business in our home were now painfully absent. Unless music was playing, the space felt unbearably silent. Sometimes a particular song would wake the grief beast, triggering waves of pain, yet I refused to turn the music off or lower the volume because it filled the empty void.

What used to be busy days filled with endless laundry, meals, work, and play are now quiet, mostly empty, and unchanging. Of course I could walk the fields, see friends, take up hobbies, volunteer at a charity shop, and so on, but there are many hours in a day. However hard it is to try and keep busy, its safer to accept the changes at your own pace. Typically, that heavy cloak of sadness will descend in the middle of the night when all those distractions are impossible.

Every day the emptiness was palpable, and it was hard to believe how just one person could create such a big void in my life. It wasn't just the feeling of loss but the realisation that everything had changed dramatically. It's not an easy thing to explain, but no doubt relatable to others who are grieving. It will take a long, long time before I stop expecting him to walk through the door.

Chapter 6

Richard

I had managed to get a handle on 2023. My husband and I had shared part of the year together, and early January had involved cautious travel plans, as we both felt they could be scuppered at any time. Unfortunately, that's exactly what happened. We had hoped to take one more trip to Australia together, but we were advised against it, gently told that a lot could happen in six weeks and to spend as much time with our family as possible. At the last minute, we headed to North Norfolk instead! It wasn't quite the same, but we both knew this would be our last holiday together. We enjoyed it as best we could with that thought weighing heavily on our minds. Our conversations were deeper, and our hugs were tighter. On the days he could manage, we strolled along the beautiful cliffs and breezy shoreline. If he needed to sleep instead, I would swim in the indoor pool, hired for my private use. I would swim furiously or float on my back, weeping silently, immersed in the music resonating around the beamed, vaulted ceiling.

It was on the day we returned when I noticed the first subtle change in his skin colour. Immediate online research confirmed my worst fears: the end was coming. I had never encountered such a definitive description of the outcome to expect from this new observation. Six weeks maximum life expectancy after the onset of jaundice, which had turned his skin slightly yellow, was spot on. I lost him four and a half weeks later.

I took some relief in the clarity of this prognosis, especially as the doctor had said the exact same thing. Instead of years of drifting towards the unknown, I now had a chance to think, plan, and brace myself for the inevitable. The reason I say 'I' and not 'we' is that he didn't want to know what I had read; he wanted to keep hope alive. It had been the thing sustaining him all this time, and he was never going to give up.

One thing I wasn't prepared for was how dramatically and quickly his body changed. He was working full-time three weeks before he died, and although some muscle loss was noticeable, he remained fit and slim. However, within two weeks, his shape altered entirely. With the strong yellow hue all over his skin, he looked like a very different man, although his hair started to grow back, which was a small comfort. I affectionately called him my yellow George Clooney. Of course, it's not about looks, but how the body could change so drastically in such a short time really took me by surprise.

Good Friday brought the loveliest spring weather, and the whole family gathered, (including Catherine and family from Australia), for an Easter egg hunt at Richard's request. It was bittersweet, knowing it would be the last time he would ever see and hear the little ones. The realisation hit me that they wouldn't play games with him anymore, which saddened me, as he was always their entertainer. Everyone kept their composure, despite the underlying awareness of the situation; we knew what was coming. Easter Saturday started positively, with an unexpected request for a curry takeaway, which he later retracted. Hours later, he uttered the haunting words that he could take it no more and had to make a call. Initially mishearing, I asked whom he wanted to call, only to be told he was ready to call time on his life.

A long, dark night followed, as we shared what we knew would be our final moments together before medical intervention became inevitable. I noticed a slight quiver in his hand around the same time the nurses observed a change in his eyes, both symptoms indicating that the morphine he was receiving was not being metabolised effectively. It became clear that a syringe driver was urgently needed to administer the medication more consistently and efficiently, before his pain escalated further. Due to the unusual circumstances, exacerbated by it being Easter Sunday, he had to be rapidly transferred under ambulance blue lights to another hospice. This unexpected move caused great distress, as we had both hoped for a calmer ending.

Easter Monday brought some comfort as he was settled and more stable. I stayed with him all day while he rested. Just as I was beginning to quietly say goodbye, unexpectedly he sat up, locked eyes with me, and gave me the biggest, most heartfelt hug. He then said all the wonderful things I had longed to hear for years. The running joke that he would keep all those hidden emotions for his deathbed had become a reality, and I was privileged to hear them.

His words were clear, concise, and filled with a depth of feeling rarely expressed. With a look in his eyes that conveyed the urgency of the moment, he shared things that are too personal to repeat but will stay with me forever. With a small wave from him and a blown kiss from me, I left the room knowing it was the final goodbye to the man I had loved for 44 years. I howled in the car with such a deep sorrow, forgetting how long the tears flowed for. The drive home was the hardest journey I had ever made, realising I would never, ever see him again.

March 2024…
Lessons learnt

…Cancer in your family is like the terrifying film adaptation of a book you were reluctant to read, but without the popcorn, and you can't leave the cinema until the credits roll. It's hard to watch, making you fidget in your chair as you fumble for a tatty tissue to mop up spilled tears and orange juice. Once you finally emerge back into the daylight, you sigh with relief that it wasn't you with cancer, but you will never, ever forget that film. You'll tell your friends about it, perhaps giving them the strength to face it should cancer or serious illness affect their lives too.

You are the lucky one who can emerge from the surreal daytime darkness into the blinding light of reality, slowly realising you have the rest of your own life to live. Or are you? Isn't this just the greatest way to teach others how to view and handle such a common and complex illness?

From this one experience of cancer in our immediate family, our children, grandchildren, extended family, and friends are learning invaluable lessons about treatments and their side effects, handling emotions across different generations, appreciating life, and maintaining a sensible outlook on their own health. It may force them to think about how they might handle it by maybe changing their diet, engaging in more exercise, not wasting energy on meaningless jobs or relationships. Managing their life well and realising they might not escape trauma one day, maybe even encouraging them to acknowledge symptoms sooner.

Stuff you can read about endlessly but witnessing

it first-hand is the best and most brutal teacher. Wasn't your most influential teacher at school the one who taught you hard and interesting facts, passionate that his knowledge was always for your own good and would help you in the future?

This is why it is vital to be open and honest when appropriate. It doesn't have to be forced down others' throats but seeing a person with cancer carrying on as best as they can is a valuable example to us all.

A memorial was pulled together rapidly, a direct cremation was arranged in the days after his passing, in order for Catherine to be able to attend as she had limited time in the UK.

A huge marquee at his beloved cricket club hosted an informal but respectful afternoon ceremony, 350 friends and family gathered in the pouring rain to remember and pay tribute to this quiet man's life and achievements.

We listened to speeches which we laughed and cried along with, dressed in bright colours and including Richards favoured coloured suits – one of his final requests being – 'that whatever you do, it must be fun and a celebration'.

Chapter 7

Final Destination

Regardless of the date Easter falls on, it now holds a significant meaning for me. Although I intend to make more effort acknowledging this time in the future for the sake of our grandchildren, this year I have planned a retreat to Herm, a twenty-minute boat ride from the Channel Island of Guernsey, close to the coast of northwest France. It's a relatively short trip from England to a place of serene beauty, reminiscent of the Caribbean in appearance. Here, I will find the same tranquillity I experienced in Australia but with just a forty-minute flight instead of seventeen hours.

I had a cosy room with a fantastic view overlooking the jetty. Each morning, I observed the tide recede, unveiling a child's haven of rock pools and sandbars that vanished as the waters returned, astonishingly able to accommodate a sizeable passenger ferry at high tide. The daily, natural phenomenon, occurring without fail, captivated me as I watched it closely without distraction, reminding me of the surrounding, incredible forces of nature we so often overlook.

The island's rhythm is dictated by this ebb and flow of the sea. Tasks are scheduled around the changing tides: buoys are checked, day trippers embark with their overstuffed suitcases delivered by tractor and trailer to their holiday cottages, mussels are collected, birds feast, and children hunt for treasures. It serves as a reminder that life continues year after year, decade after decade, with little change except for technology either aiding or abetting the process. It puts our individual positions on this earth into perspective, whether we live on a massive island like Australia, or a tiny one like Herm.

Every day on this island jewel, measuring one and a half miles by half a mile in size, I've spent around three hours completing the full coastal and beach paths. Although the entire circuit can be done in two hours, I have taken my time, often exploring different routes and often covering the same paths. The cliff walks are rugged and, though they occasionally test my fear of heights, the paths are mostly smooth and well-maintained, offering outstanding views of the sea at every turn.

The cliffs of the south, famous for their puffins, stand in stark contrast to the powdery beaches in the north, where turquoise waters lap against the sand and the occasional rock formations that must be scrambled over to reach the next stretch. The island's ample heathland and hills make it an ideal family holiday destination, whether for a week or a weekend. Two beach cafés, beautifully stocked, maintained and unobtrusive, blend seamlessly into the landscape, providing perfect rest stops during a hike. They encourage even reluctant people like me to see what's around the next corner after a well-deserved drink and bite to eat.

Reflecting on the past eleven and a half months, I find myself vividly recalling the events of a year ago – the build-up, the last days, and the funeral. These memories are constantly with me. I pore over videos of the memorial, feeling equally sad and proud, indulging my emotions once again. However, I now feel ready to draw a faint, wobbly line under my grief and push on, or should I say, *'Ramble On'*.

As the one-year anniversary approaches, Richard's death feels more distant and permanent. Counting the months keeps it feeling recent, but I know if he were to walk through the front door now, my life would return to normal almost immediately. It's akin to marking the age of a newborn in months, holding on to their newness until they turn one-year-old and become fully integrated into everyday life. A year seals the deal that this is my reality now, whether I like it or not. There will be no more shared memories with Richard; they will be just mine. It also takes longer each time to scroll back through my phone's photos and messages to when he was alive. I miss the shared laughter, gossip, and the spontaneous affection, no hugs, kisses, or even text messages to break the silence of my day. I still send his contact a kiss every few days to keep our last conversations close at hand, always feeling sad to see my simple message undelivered. But at least today, I cried only once and smiled five times, the complete opposite to a year ago.

April 2024…
Lilies and a rainbow

…On one of the anniversaries of last year, laden with sombre memories, I decided to do some volunteering. The experience left me feeling upbeat and fulfilled. However, knowing the evening would likely be poignant, I stopped for petrol on the way home and grabbed a bottle of wine in anticipation.

Still riding high from my day's work, I approached the till where a cashier I'd never met, unaware of my circumstances, kindly offered me a free bunch of lilies that were on sale, still with closed buds. I expressed gratitude, as I was deeply moved by this timely gesture, especially given that lilies hold such significance of loss. I managed to hold back tears until I reached my car.

Back home, composed once more, I sat at my computer with a view across fields opposite. I noticed dark clouds gathering on the horizon, unexpected rain falling, and then a clear, beautiful rainbow forming, landing directly on the tree under which we were interviewed by the BBC several months earlier about Richard's cancer treatment. Through tears and a mix of emotions, I hurriedly snapped a photo from the front door, only to find the rainbow had faded completely by the time I returned inside.

These signs, or whatever they may be, come at the most incredible times. Whether they are coincidence or something more, they are always profoundly moving – bringing tears and smiles in equal measure, lifting spirits and offering hope. As I've mentioned before, I've encountered quite a few of these moments, and their impact never fails to astonish me.

Dreams hold a similar power. Recently, I had a vivid one where Richard walked through the front door. I saw his shoes, the clothes he was wearing, heard his voice react to an overeager dog – and then I woke up, tears streaming down my face. It's hard to fathom how these dreams unfold, but this one, despite the sadness it brought, also made me smile. In that brief moment, life felt normal again, as if the past eleven months had been a bad dream, and Richard was back home – the best split second of recent memory.

A year has passed, 364 days of waking up alone, and all the official matters are settled, so my life is normal again, apparently. Yet, I still expect you to come home. Our home is different now. I have fewer dishes in the kitchen and enough towels in the bathroom for one. There's food in the freezer you would hate and hooks in the hall that aren't bulging with coats for all weathers. Even the shoe rack has spaces. The half empty wardrobe only has pretty things – no suits, ties, belts, or garish shirts anymore.

No mud stains on the carpet, no curry leftovers. The open jar of pickled onions in the fridge looks suspicious, but since you were the last one to dip your fingers in it, it remains there. The one-pint milk container still looks ridiculous. The lone potato sprouts, and I take the frozen loaf of bread out one slice at a time. At least I can have chicken three days in a row if I like, and I don't hear constant cricket on the television anymore. Yet, I no longer wait for the call to pick you up or wonder if you're hungry after spending hours cooking, only for you to forget to text me again.

An organised home, every wife's dream, is now a haunting reminder of widowhood. The dishwasher smells from lack of use, the washing machine rarely runs, and the iron gathers dust. I would rather have you here, with mud on your boots and kisses tinged with pickled onion, stubble grazing my cheek, and your voice mingling in the air we once shared. I no longer have to ask you to reach the top shelf anymore, as I've rearranged the few things I use to be within my grasp.

The black tulips are in the garden again. You once bought me a hundred bulbs, and they became a symbol for us. Last year, I placed one of the only two remaining next to your bed. Today, the sole tulip that has bloomed this year stands above your ashes, beneath your picture.

Every day, I walk across the fields to place a stone on one of the cairns Richard started building after his terminal diagnosis. (Cairns are piles of stones historically used as memorials or navigational aids). He had built five small cairns in the corner of nearby fields, next to a path opposite our house, adding a few stones to each cairn he created on his daily walk. As a family, we were encouraged to add a stone whenever we passed by, and the grandchildren painted them and adorned them with flowers. This tradition gave us a place to go as a family after his passing, a practice we've all continued to uphold.

I never thought I would get through even one week without you, so I suppose I've done well. Time doesn't heal, but it has given me space to think, weigh things up, and slowly conclude that I can survive. My mind will reluctantly, but naturally, adjust if I let it. People say that getting past the first anniversary of everything is supposed to be a good thing, but I think it just highlights how much you have missed out on. I'll see how I feel this time next year.

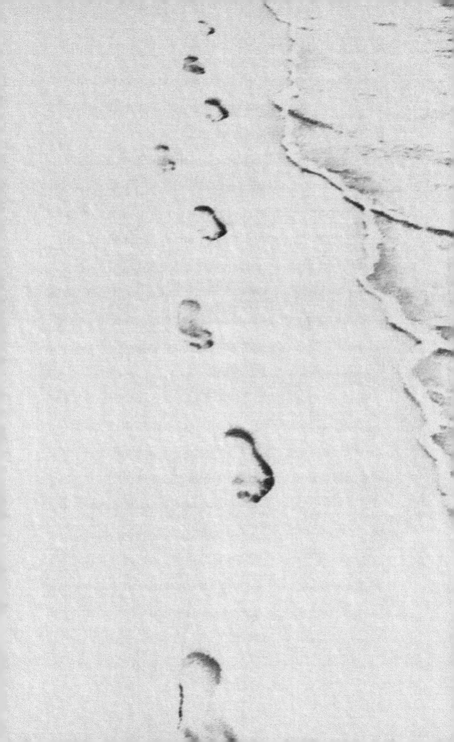

Things I have learnt on my travels:

- When swimming in the shallows, if a lump of seaweed suddenly moves fast, it is not seaweed!

- There are at least 15 ways to make a ham and cheese toastie, and they are not all good.

- Never underestimate the persistence of the Australian fly, mosquito, or sun.

- Eating aeroplane meals is like a sliding tile puzzle. It takes patience and practice.

- You are not allowed to paint your nails on a plane because of the fumes, apparently.

- Your passport will not jump out of your zipped bag, so there is no need to check it every five minutes.

- Australian TV is hit and miss in hotels, and vintage Baywatch is not a healthy binge watch.

- Never trust the brakes of a hired bike and choose your helmet wisely!

- Always wear a supportive bra at airports!

"Try not to let grief consume you, it is a necessary but dangerous beast. Allow it to be your constant companion, not your master."

Acknowledgements

The Royal Marsden Cancer Charity
With heartfelt thanks and gratitude for all the
care Richard received. The compassion and
professionalism we were given was outstanding.
I will continue to support your work and carry on
where Richard left off.

Royal Alfred Seafarers' Society
The amazing support you gave during such a hard
time will never be forgotten by my family and me.
You looked after all of us, especially in that last
week, with the dedication and love that reflects the
ethos of this incredible society. Thank you.

Banstead Cricket Club
Thank you to all our friends from the club Richard
called his second home. I, however, called it his
first! The support and energy so many of you gave
in arranging his memorial in such a short time is
something we will never, ever forget.

*I may have a sad story to tell but I do not have a sad
life with all of you a part of it.*